Contributing Author
Kassie Lewis

Editorial Project Manager
Mara Ellen Guckian

Managing Editors
Karen J. Goldfluss M.S. Ed.
Ina Massler Levin M.A.

Illustrators
Kevin Barnes
Reneé Christine Yates

Cover Design
Kevin Barnes
CJae Froshay

Art Manager
Kevin Barnes

Art Director
CJae Froshay

Imaging
Craig L. Gunnell
Ralph Olmedo, Jr.

Publisher
Mary Dupuy Smith, M.S. Ed.

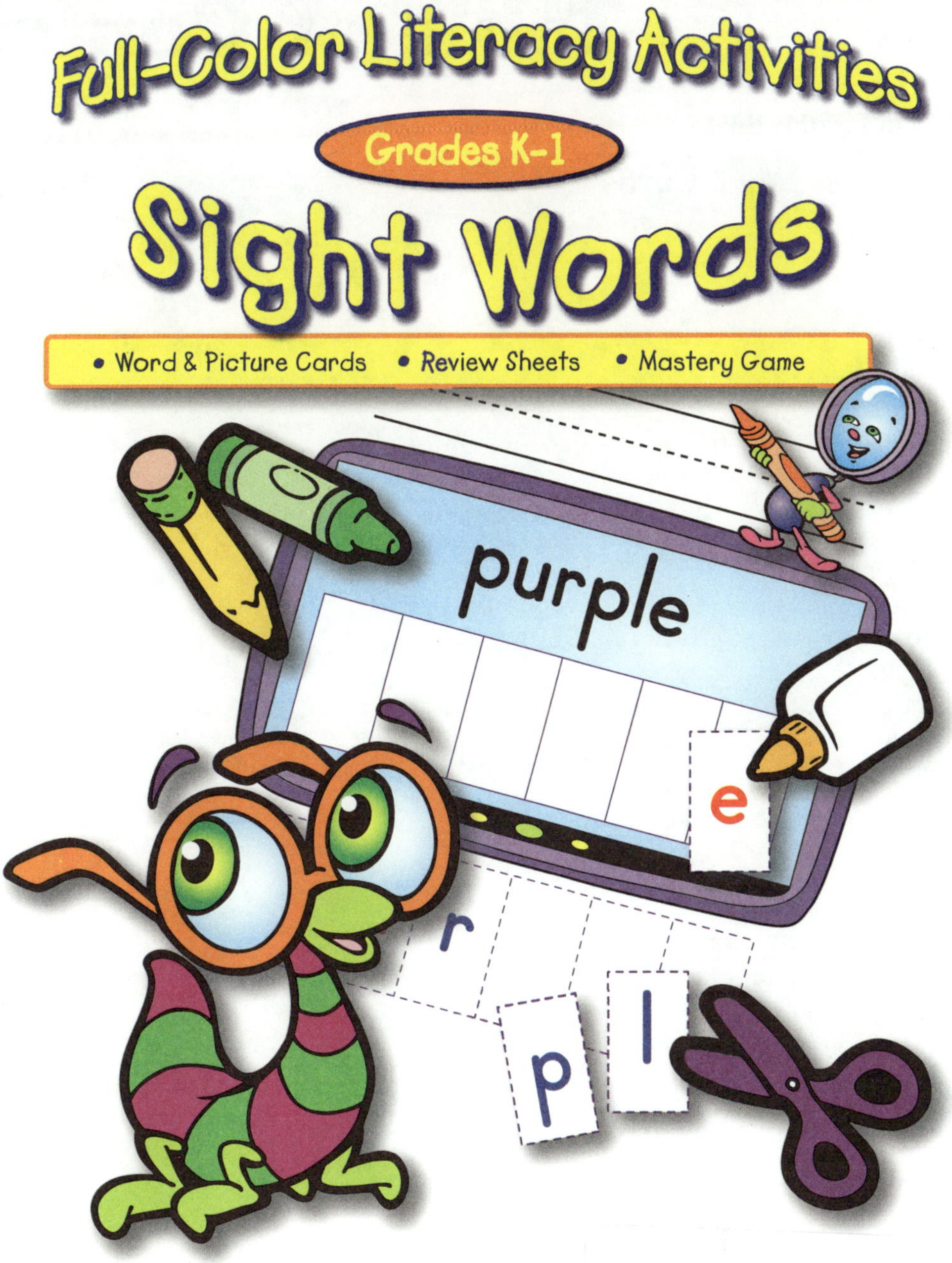

Full-Color Literacy Activities

Grades K-1

Sight Words

• Word & Picture Cards • Review Sheets • Mastery Game

Author
Renee Liles

Teacher Created Resources, Inc.
6421 Industry Way
Westminster, CA 92683
www.teachercreated.com.
ISBN-1-4206-3174-8
©2005 Teacher Created Resources, Inc.
Made in U.S.A.

Table of Contents

Table of Contents *(Cont.)*

Introduction

It is time to start learning to read and write words, but where do we begin? Many of the most frequently used words, commonly called *sight words*, do not follow standard decoding rules. Further, they are not nouns and can not be easily illustrated. Word flash cards help, but research has proven that young students learn best with hands-on practice. This simple, easy-to–use book will give students the much-needed practice recognizing and spelling 60 of the most common sight words.

For simplicity, these sight words are introduced alphabetically. Grouping words with similar beginning letters helps students with letter recognition. Grouping words in this manner also encourages students to look beyond the initial letter of the word, thus focusing more on the spelling of the whole word.

Students also need practice reading from left to right when arranging letters to form words. The color cards and puzzle-like quality of the activities will engage students and make sight words more fun to learn. Additionally, activities like cutting, pasting, sorting, and printing reinforce fine motor skill development.

How to Use this Book

The 60 word cards provided in *Full-Color Literacy Centers for Sight Words* can be used in small groups, as center work or individually to meet student needs. (**Teacher Note:** Reproduce the word card pages before cutting. That way, they can be used as additional worksheets for extra practice.)

Word Cards for Center Use

The word cards (pages 5–123) need little preparation. On all cards, consonants are blue and vowels are red. All letter cards are lowercase. Simply cut out the word cards and letter pieces and laminate them for added durability. The directions and name lines on the word card pages can be discarded when using the cards in the center. Place each prepared word card and its letters in an envelope or resealable bag and label it. Store the cards in the center in a box or other container. (**Teacher Note:** One-and two-letter word cards have additional, unrelated letters. Instruct children to choose the correct letters to spell the word.)

Worksheets

The reproducible worksheets (pages 125-152) review groups of sight words. Each grouping is listed under the page title. Practice these sight words first with the full-color word cards. Once students are familiar with the sight words listed under the page title, that worksheet can be used as a center, a class worksheet, or as homework. In the beginning, students will need assistance with directions. These worksheets work best as teacher-directed activities and can be used for large or small groups. To use a worksheet in a center, copy the page and laminate it or put it in a page protector. Adult supervision may be needed to read directions. Have students write on the laminate or the page protector using thin, dry-erase pens. Wipe with a damp paper towel to erase when completed. Using these worksheets as part of a center allows students many opportunities to succeed at the task. Special instructions for certain activities are given in a *Center Note* at the bottom of the worksheet.

Center Cards and Picture Cards

Once students have begun to master the 60 sight words, the sentence cards and picture cards (pages 153–157) and the Sight Word Master game (pages 161–173) will reinforce the words through fun and creative play. A student can use from 6 to 60 cards for the game.

Name: _______________________________

✂ Cut out the letters to make the word.

🧴 Glue or place the correct letter in each box.

🖍 Write the word.

a

e c a

✂ Cut out the letters to make the word.

🍶 Glue or place the correct letter in each box.

🖍 Write the word.

all

Name: ______________________________

✂ Cut out the letters to make the word.

🧴 Glue or place the correct letter in each box.

🖍 Write the word.

am

Name: ____

✂ Cut out the letters to make the word.

🖊 Glue or place the correct letter in each box.

🖍 Write the word.

an

n e a

Teacher
Created
Resources

Teacher
Created
Resources

Teacher
Created
Resources

Teacher
Created
Resources

Teacher
Created
Resources

Teacher
Created
Resources

Teacher
Created
Resources

Teacher
Created
Resources

Teacher
Created
Resources

Teacher
Created
Resources

Teacher
Created
Resources

Teacher
Created
Resources

Teacher
Created
Resources

Teacher
Created
Resources

Teacher
Created
Resources

Teacher
Created
Resources

Teacher
Created
Resources

Teacher
Created
Resources

Teacher
Created
Resources

Teacher
Created
Resources

Teacher
Created
Resources

Teacher
Created
Resources

Teacher
Created
Resources

Teacher
Created
Resources

Teacher
Created
Resources

Teacher
Created
Resources

Teacher
Created
Resources

Teacher
Created
Resources

Teacher
Created
Resources

Teacher
Created
Resources

Teacher
Created
Resources

Teacher
Created
Resources

Cut out the letters to make the word.

Glue or place the correct letter in each box.

Write the word.

and

d a n

 Cut out the letters to make the word.

 Glue or place the correct letter in each box.

 Write the word.

are

r a e

Name: _______________________________

Cut out the letters to make the word.

Glue or place the correct letter in each box.

Write the word.

- Cut out the letters to make the word.
- Glue or place the correct letter in each box.
- Write the word.

✂ Cut out the letters to make the word.

🍼 Glue or place the correct letter in each box.

🖍 Write the word.

Name: _______________________________

 Cut out the letters to make the word.

 Glue or place the correct letter in each box.

 Write the word.

Name: ___________________________________

Cut out the letters to make the word.

Glue or place the correct letter in each box.

Write the word.

Name: ____

✂ Cut out the letters to make the word.

🧴 Glue or place the correct letter in each box.

🖍 Write the word.

 Cut out the letters to make the word.

 Glue or place the correct letter in each box.

Write the word.

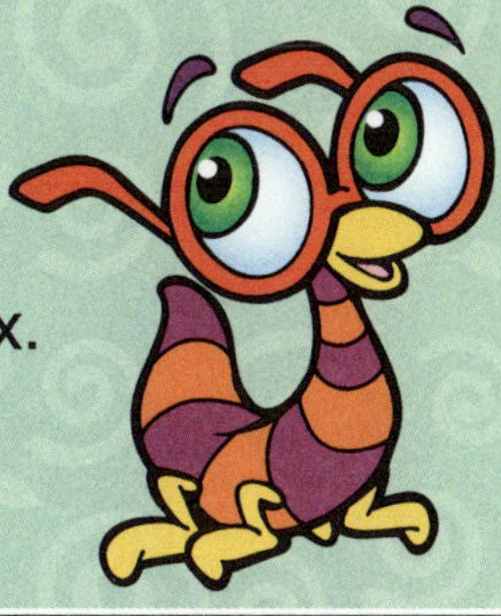

each

e h c a

 Cut out the letters to make the word.

 Glue or place the correct letter in each box.

 Write the word.

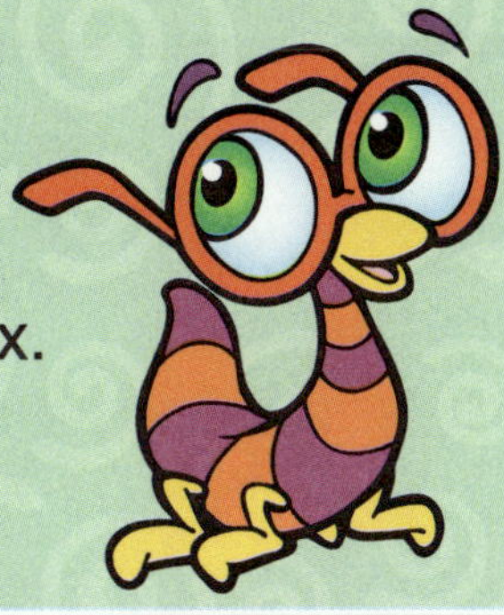

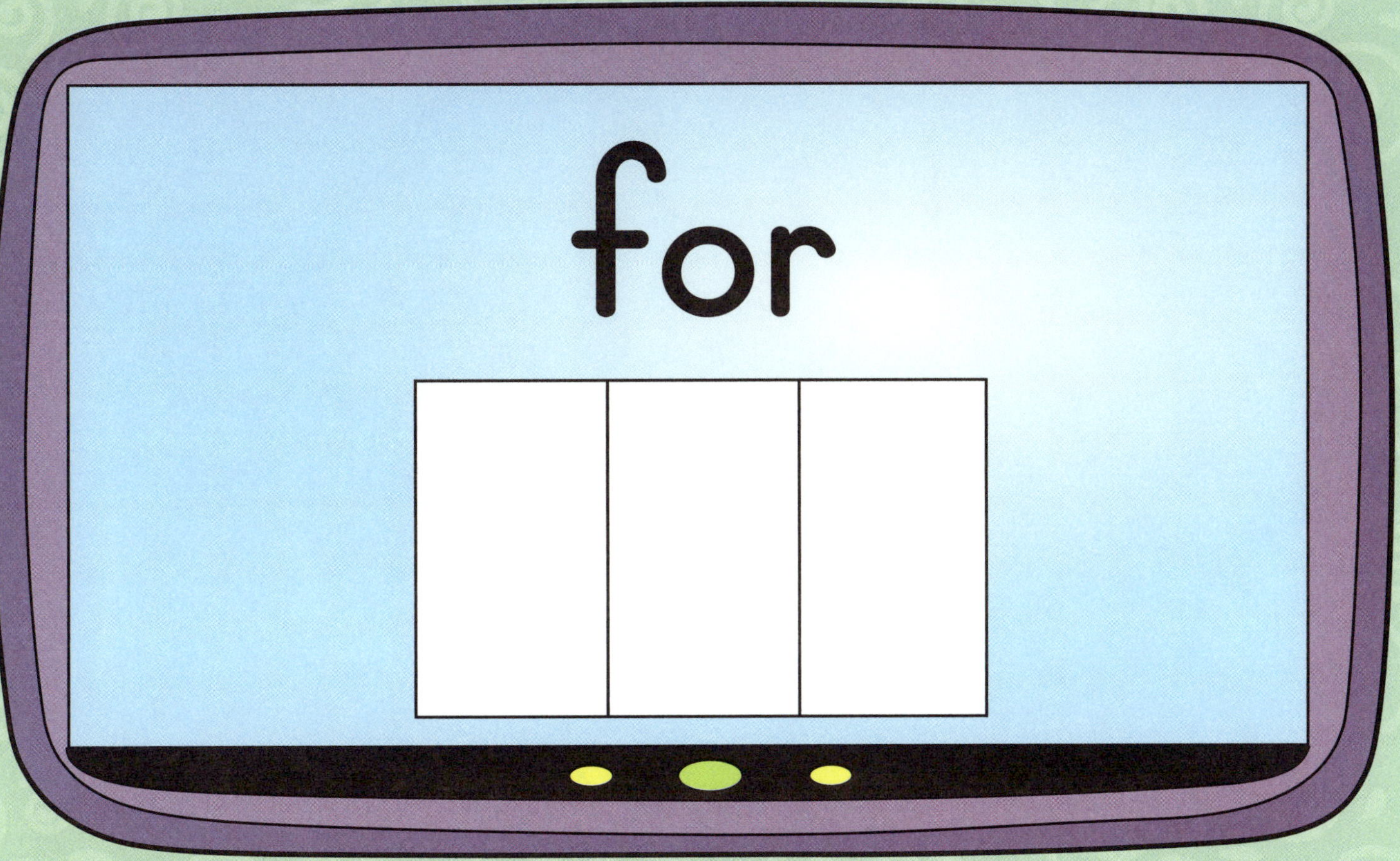

 Cut out the letters to make the word.

 Glue or place the correct letter in each box.

 Write the word.

from

m f r o

Cut out the letters to make the word.

Glue or place the correct letter in each box.

Write the word.

go

o a g

Cut out the letters to make the word.

Glue or place the correct letter in each box.

Write the word.

 Cut out the letters to make the word.

 Glue or place the correct letter in each box.

 Write the word.

here

h r e e

Name: ___________________________________

 Cut out the letters to make the word.

 Glue or place the correct letter in each box.

Write the word.

h   s   i

 Cut out the letters to make the word.

 Glue or place the correct letter in each box.

 Write the word.

if

f   t   i

 Cut out the letters to make the word.

 Glue or place the correct letter in each box.

 Write the word.

in

n m i

Cut out the letters to make the word.

Glue or place the correct letter in each box.

Write the word.

 Cut out the letters to make the word.

Glue or place the correct letter in each box.

Write the word.

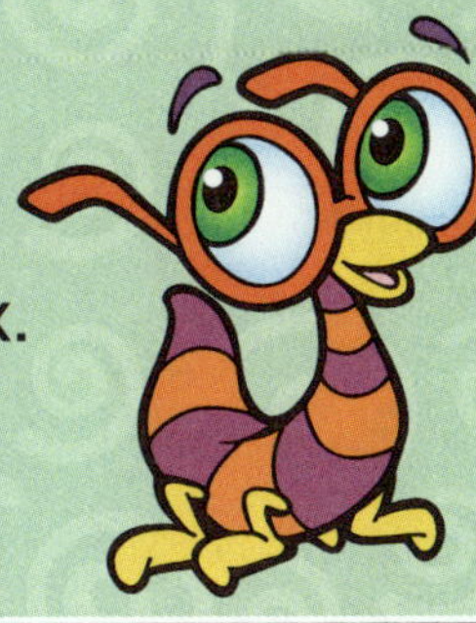

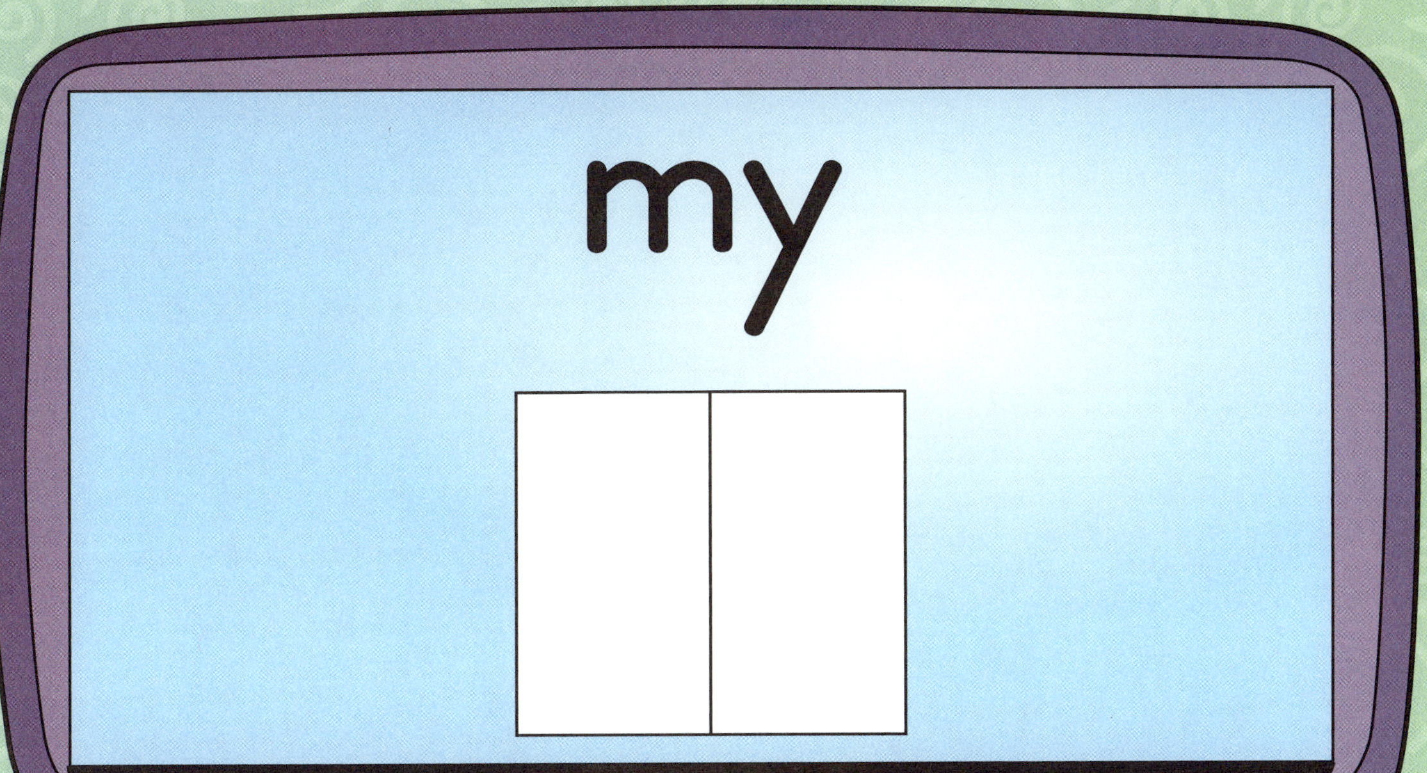

- ✂ Cut out the letters to make the word.
- 🍶 Glue or place the correct letter in each box.
- 🖍 Write the word.

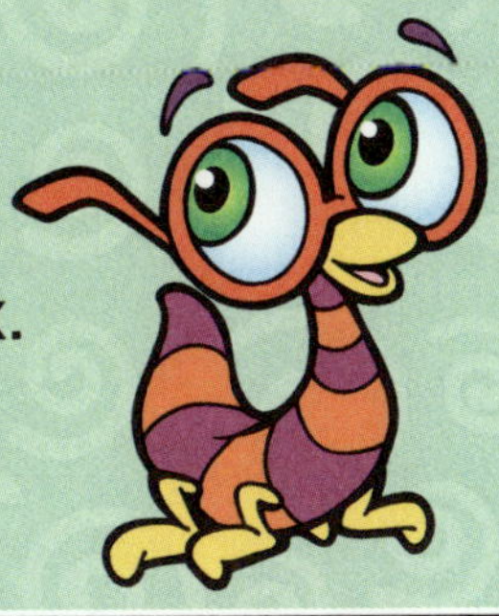

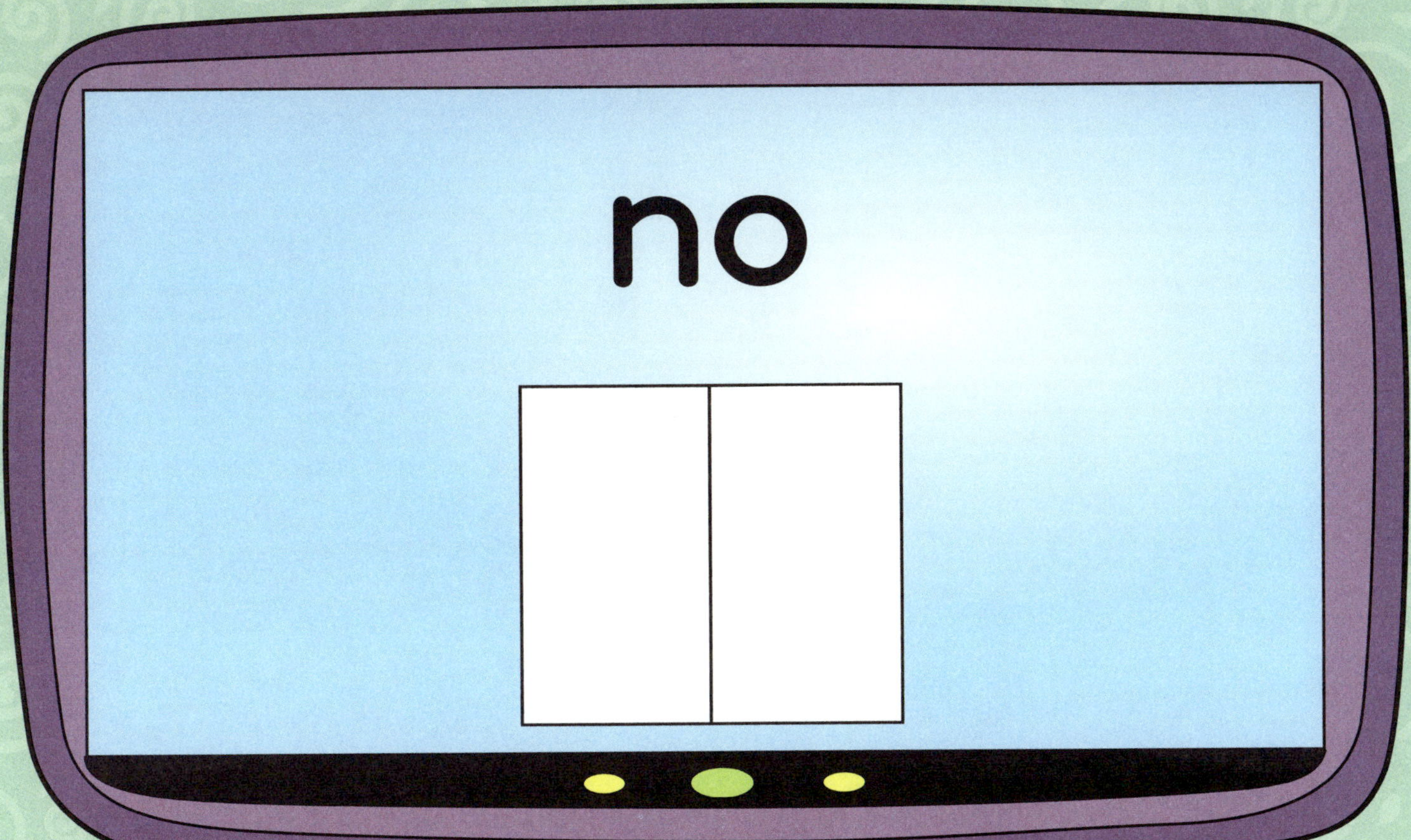

Name: ___________________________

 Cut out the letters to make the word.

 Glue or place the correct letter in each box.

 Write the word.

not

 Cut out the letters to make the word.

 Glue or place the correct letter in each box.

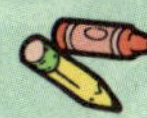 Write the word.

of

f v o

Cut out the letters to make the word.

Glue or place the correct letter in each box.

Write the word.

Name: ___________________________________

✂ Cut out the letters to make the word.

🖊 Glue or place the correct letter in each box.

🖍 Write the word.

play

y l p a

Cut out the letters to make the word.

Glue or place the correct letter in each box.

Write the word.

said

d i s a

Name: _______________________________

 Cut out the letters to make the word.

 Glue or place the correct letter in each box.

Write the word.

Name: _______________________________

✂ Cut out the letters to make the word.

🖌 Glue or place the correct letter in each box.

🖍 Write the word.

stop

✂ Cut out the letters to make the word.

🍶 Glue or place the correct letter in each box.

🖍 Write the word.

Name: ______________________________

Cut out the letters to make the word.

Glue or place the correct letter in each box.

Write the word.

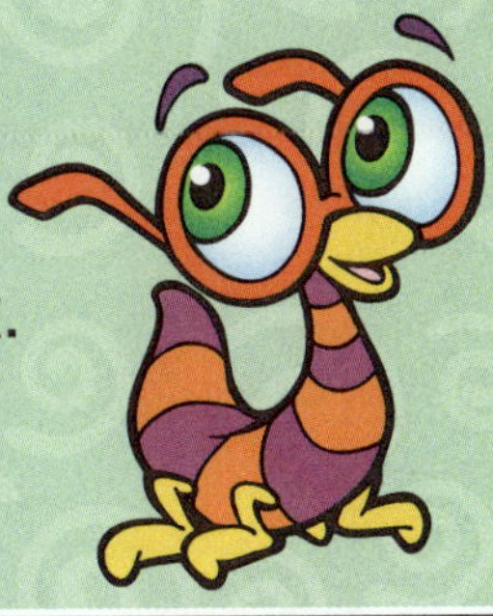

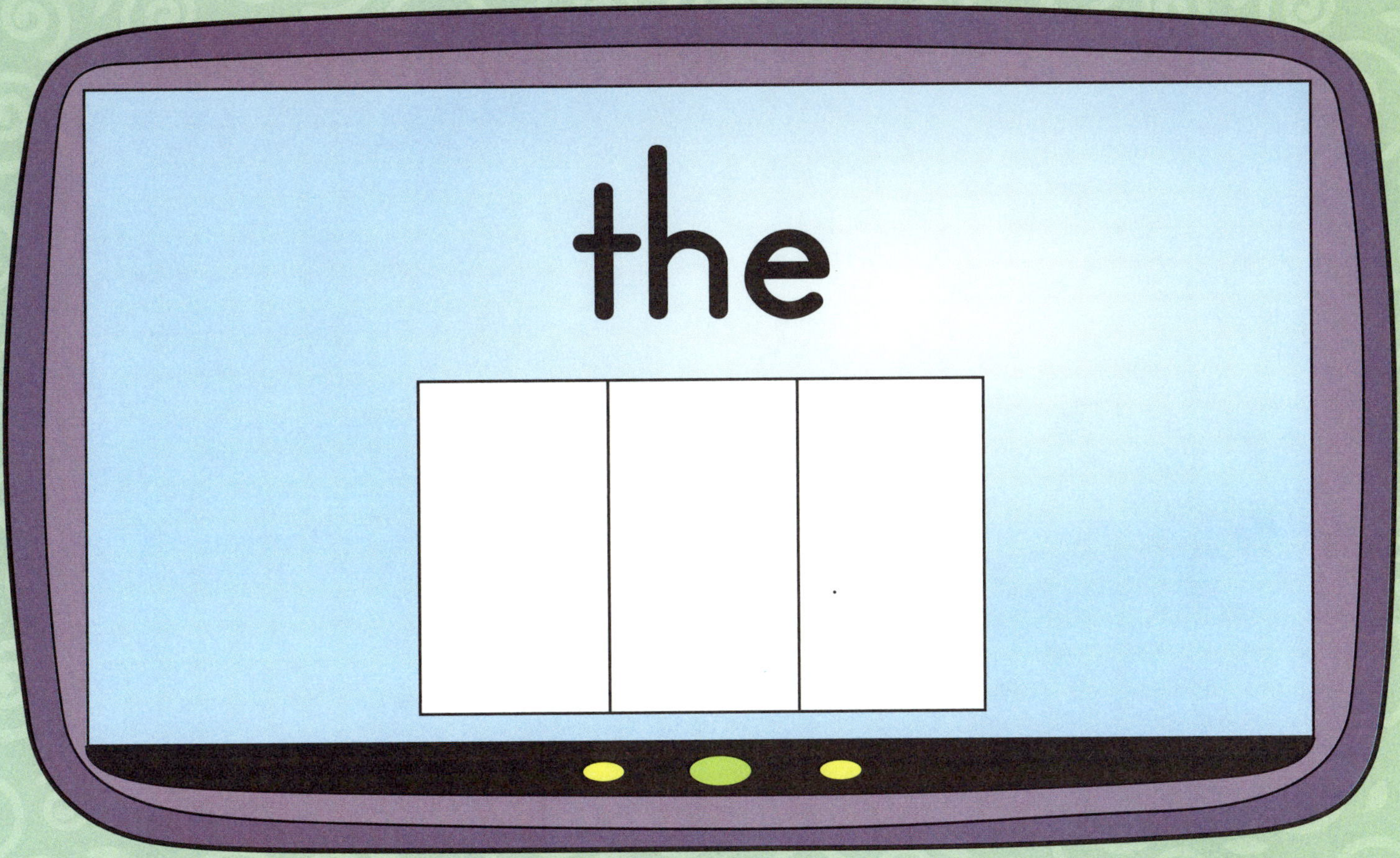

h t e

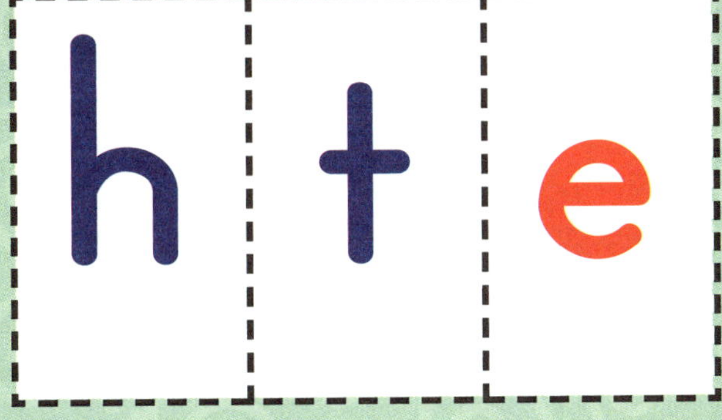

Cut out the letters and make this word

Glue or place the correct letter in the box.

Write the word.

there

h t e e r

Cut out the letters and make this word

Glue or place the correct letter in the box.

Write the word.

Name: _______________________________

✂ Cut out the letters to make the word.

🧴 Glue or place the correct letter in each box.

🖍 Write the word.

this

Cut out the letters to make the word.

Glue or place the correct letter in each box.

Write the word.

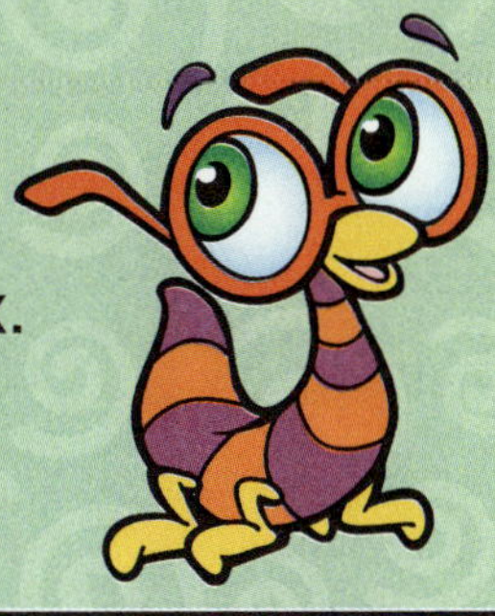

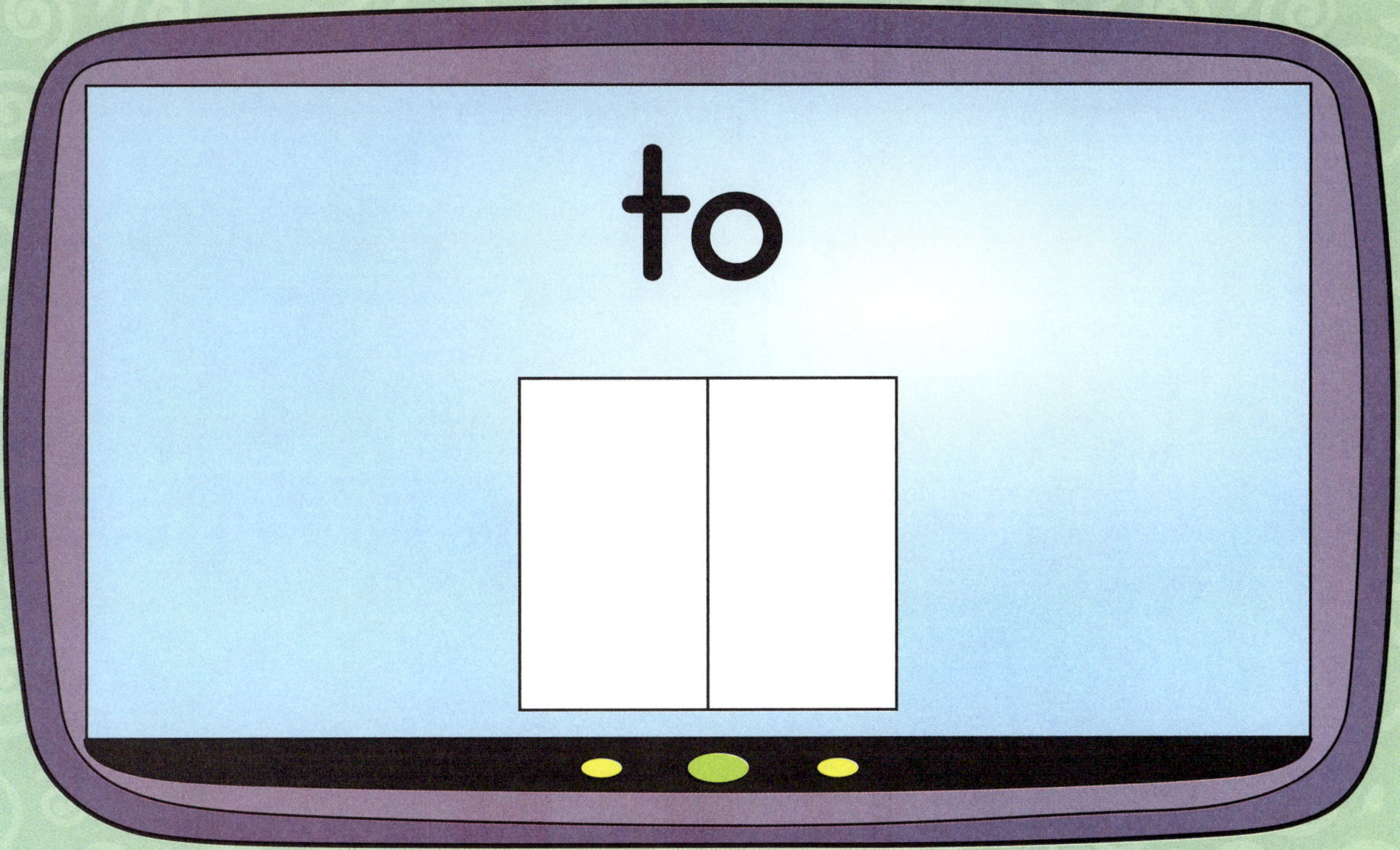

to

Name: _______________________________

✂ Cut out the letters to make the word.

🖌 Glue or place the correct letter in each box.

🖍 Write the word.

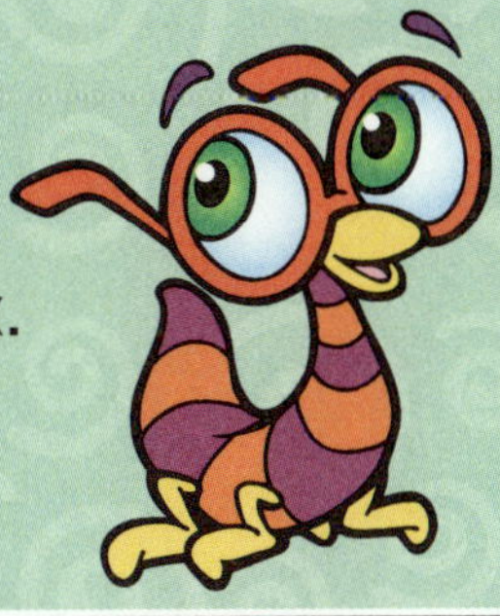

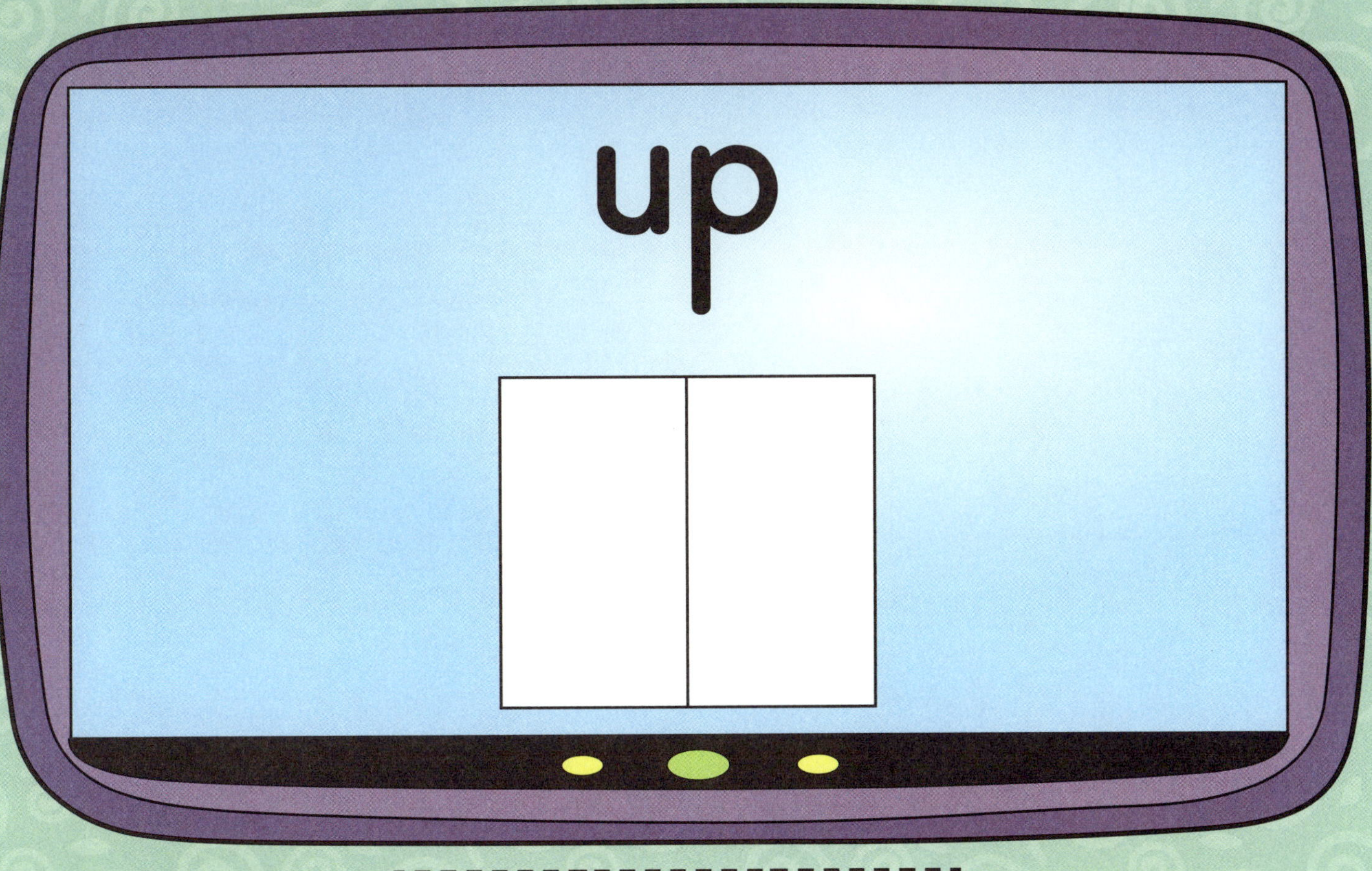

Name: _______________________________

Cut out the letters to make the word.

Glue or place the correct letter in each box.

Write the word.

- Cut out the letters to make the word.
- Glue or place the correct letter in each box.
- Write the word.

were

e e r w

Cut out the letters to make the word.

Glue or place the correct letter in each box.

Write the word.

✂ Cut out the letters to make the word.

🥛 Glue or place the correct letter in each box.

🖍 Write the word.

Teacher
Created
Resources

Teacher
Created
Resources

Teacher
Created
Resources

Teacher
Created
Resources

Teacher
Created
Resources

Teacher
Created
Resources

Teacher
Created
Resources

Teacher
Created
Resources

Teacher
Created
Resources

Teacher
Created
Resources

Teacher
Created
Resources

Teacher
Created
Resources

Teacher
Created
Resources

Teacher
Created
Resources

Teacher
Created
Resources

Teacher
Created
Resources

Teacher
Created
Resources

Teacher
Created
Resources

Teacher
Created
Resources

Teacher
Created
Resources

Teacher
Created
Resources

Teacher
Created
Resources

Teacher
Created
Resources

Teacher
Created
Resources

Teacher
Created
Resources

Teacher
Created
Resources

Teacher
Created
Resources

Teacher
Created
Resources

Teacher
Created
Resources

Teacher
Created
Resources

Teacher
Created
Resources

Teacher
Created
Resources

Name: _______________________________

✂ Cut out the letters to make the word.

🧴 Glue or place the correct letter in each box.

🖍 Write the word.

Name: _______________________________

Cut out the letters to make the word.
Glue or place the correct letter in each box.
Write the word.

it

t + i

 Cut out the letters to make the word.

 Glue or place the correct letter in each box.

 Write the word.

she

h s e

Teacher
Created
Resources

Teacher
Created
Resources

Teacher
Created
Resources

Teacher
Created
Resources

Teacher
Created
Resources

Teacher
Created
Resources

Teacher
Created
Resources

Teacher
Created
Resources

Teacher
Created
Resources

Teacher
Created
Resources

Teacher
Created
Resources

Teacher
Created
Resources

Teacher
Created
Resources

Teacher
Created
Resources

Teacher
Created
Resources

Teacher
Created
Resources

Teacher
Created
Resources

Teacher
Created
Resources

Teacher
Created
Resources

Teacher
Created
Resources

Teacher
Created
Resources

Teacher
Created
Resources

Teacher
Created
Resources

Teacher
Created
Resources

Teacher
Created
Resources

Teacher
Created
Resources

Teacher
Created
Resources

Teacher
Created
Resources

Teacher
Created
Resources

Teacher
Created
Resources

Teacher
Created
Resources

Teacher
Created
Resources

Cut out the letters to make the word.

Glue or place the correct letter in each box.

Write the word.

they

y h t e

✂ Cut out the letters to make the word.

🖊 Glue or place the correct letter in each box.

✏ Write the word.

Teacher Created Resources

Name: ____

Cut out the letters to make the word.

Glue or place the correct letter in each box.

Write the word.

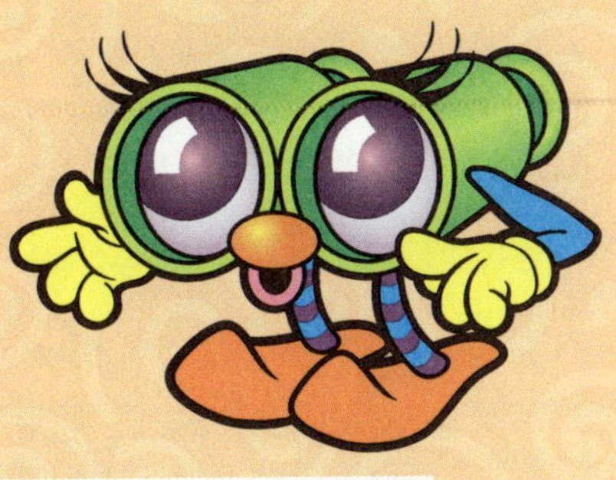

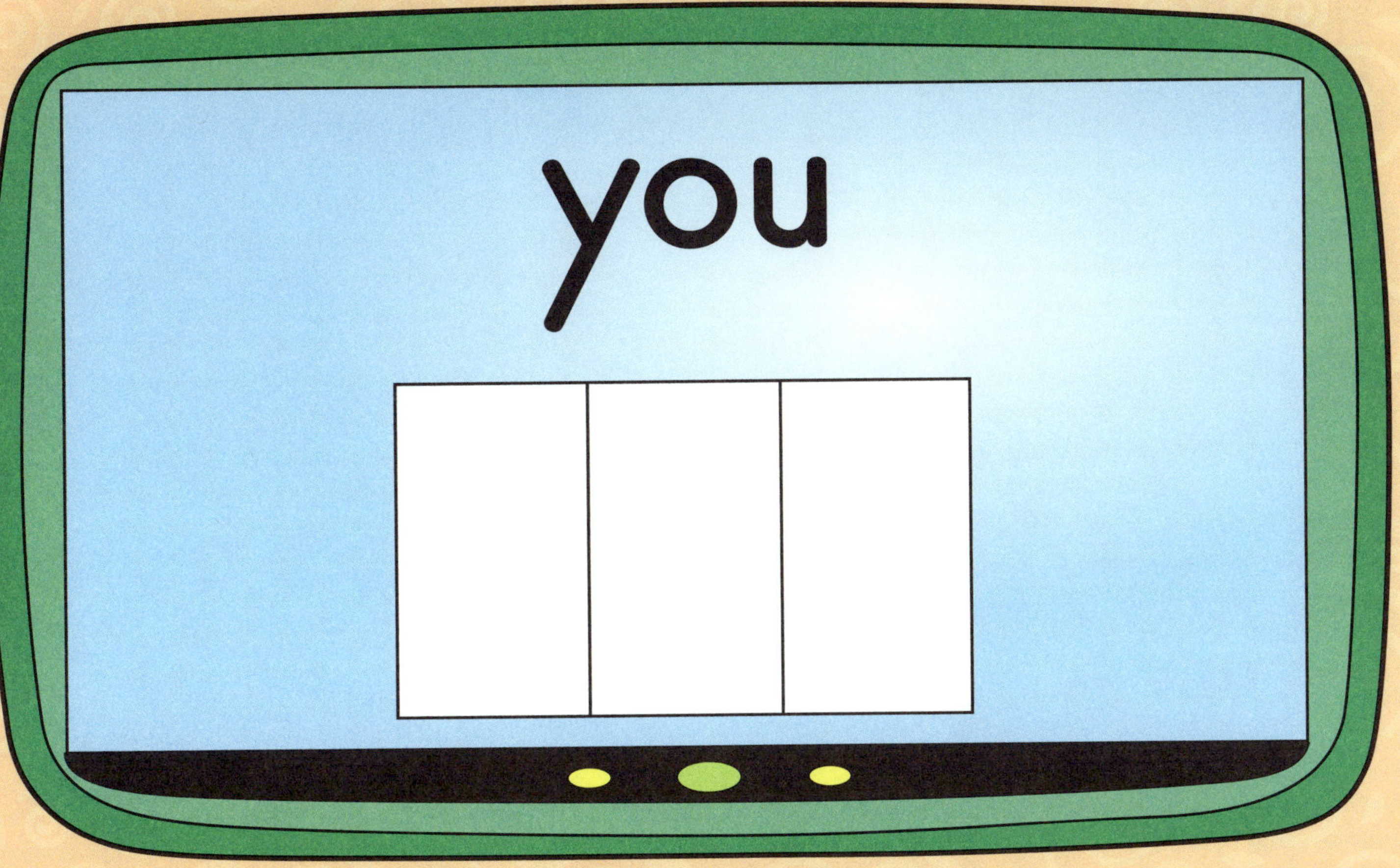

u	y	o

Name: _______________________________

black

k a c b l

Cut out the letters to make the word.

Glue or place the correct letter in each box.

Write the word.

Name: _______________________________

 Cut out the letters to make the word.

 Glue or place the correct letter in each box.

 Write the word.

brown

n r o w b

✂ Cut out the letters to make the word.

🧴 Glue or place the correct letter in each box.

🖍 Write the word.

gray

Name: _______________________________

✂ Cut out the letters to make the word.

🖌 Glue or place the correct letter in each box.

🖍 Write the word.

green

Teacher
Created
Resources

Teacher
Created
Resources

Teacher
Created
Resources

Teacher
Created
Resources

Teacher
Created
Resources

Teacher
Created
Resources

Teacher
Created
Resources

Teacher
Created
Resources

Teacher
Created
Resources

Teacher
Created
Resources

Teacher
Created
Resources

Teacher
Created
Resources

Teacher
Created
Resources

Teacher
Created
Resources

Teacher
Created
Resources

Teacher
Created
Resources

Teacher
Created
Resources

Teacher
Created
Resources

Teacher
Created
Resources

Teacher
Created
Resources

Teacher
Created
Resources

Teacher
Created
Resources

Teacher
Created
Resources

Teacher
Created
Resources

Teacher
Created
Resources

Teacher
Created
Resources

Teacher
Created
Resources

Teacher
Created
Resources

Teacher
Created
Resources

Teacher
Created
Resources

Teacher
Created
Resources

Teacher
Created
Resources

Name: _______________________________________

Cut out the letters to make the word.

Glue or place the correct letter in each box.

Write the word.

orange

o a e r n g

Teacher
Created
Resources

Teacher
Created
Resources

Teacher
Created
Resources

Teacher
Created
Resources

Teacher
Created
Resources

Teacher
Created
Resources

Teacher
Created
Resources

Teacher
Created
Resources

Teacher
Created
Resources

Teacher
Created
Resources

Teacher
Created
Resources

Teacher
Created
Resources

Teacher
Created
Resources

Teacher
Created
Resources

Teacher
Created
Resources

Teacher
Created
Resources

Teacher
Created
Resources

Teacher
Created
Resources

Teacher
Created
Resources

Teacher
Created
Resources

Teacher
Created
Resources

Teacher
Created
Resources

Teacher
Created
Resources

Teacher
Created
Resources

Teacher
Created
Resources

Teacher
Created
Resources

Teacher
Created
Resources

Teacher
Created
Resources

Teacher
Created
Resources

Teacher
Created
Resources

Teacher
Created
Resources

Teacher
Created
Resources

Name: _______________________________

✂️ Cut out the letters to make the word.

🧴 Glue or place the correct letter in each box.

🖍️ Write the word.

Name: ___________________________

- Cut out the letters to make the word.
- Glue or place the correct letter in each box.
- Write the word.

purple

p r e u l p

Name: ________________________

 Cut out the letters to make the word.

 Glue or place the correct letter in each box.

 Write the word.

red

Teacher
Created
Resources

Teacher
Created
Resources

Teacher
Created
Resources

Teacher
Created
Resources

Teacher
Created
Resources

Teacher
Created
Resources

Teacher
Created
Resources

Teacher
Created
Resources

Teacher
Created
Resources

Teacher
Created
Resources

Teacher
Created
Resources

Teacher
Created
Resources

Teacher
Created
Resources

Teacher
Created
Resources

Teacher
Created
Resources

Teacher
Created
Resources

Teacher
Created
Resources

Teacher
Created
Resources

Teacher
Created
Resources

Teacher
Created
Resources

Teacher
Created
Resources

Teacher
Created
Resources

Teacher
Created
Resources

Teacher
Created
Resources

Teacher
Created
Resources

Teacher
Created
Resources

Teacher
Created
Resources

Teacher
Created
Resources

Teacher
Created
Resources

Teacher
Created
Resources

Teacher
Created
Resources

Teacher
Created
Resources

✂ Cut out the letters to make the word.

🧴 Glue or place the correct letter in each box.

🖍 Write the word.

white

Cut out the letters to make the word.

Glue or place the correct letter in each box.

Write the word.

yellow

l l w e y o

Wrangling Sight Words

Put a yellow circle around *all*. (all) Put a purple circle around *a*. (a)

Put a red circle around *am*. (am) Put a green circle around *an*. (an)

Put a blue circle around *and*. (and) Put an orange circle around *are*. (are)

all   am   and

are   a

an

Trace, write, and read the sight words.

a _______________   an _______________

all _______________   and _______________

am _______________   are _______________

Name: ______________________________

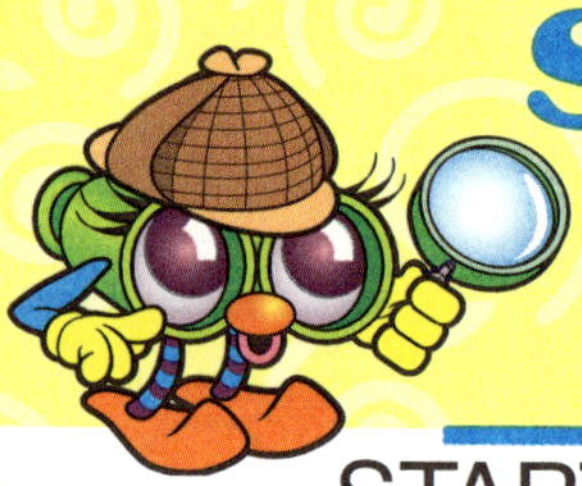

Sight Word Detective

a, all, am, an, and, are

Follow the word *are* from start to finish.

START

are	are	are	all	am
am	and	are	an	all
a	all	are	are	an
and	a	and	are	FINISH

Trace the words. How many times do you see each sight word in the puzzle?

a	2	am		an	
all		and		are	

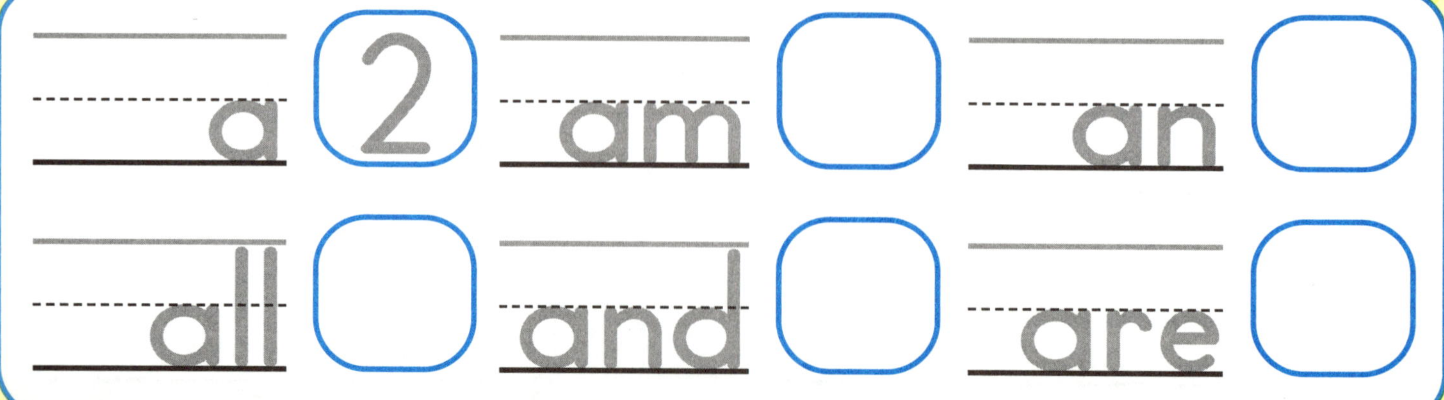

Find the Same

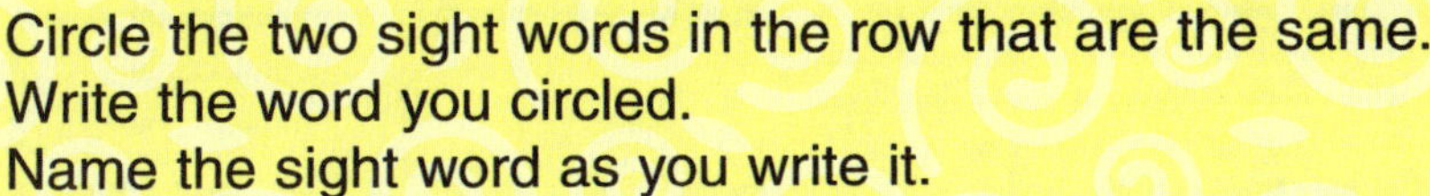

as, at, be, by, but, can

Circle the two sight words in the row that are the same.
Write the word you circled.
Name the sight word as you write it.

as	at	as	_________
can	can	by	_________
be	by	by	_________
but	can	but	_________
at	at	but	_________
be	be	at	_________

Name: ____________________

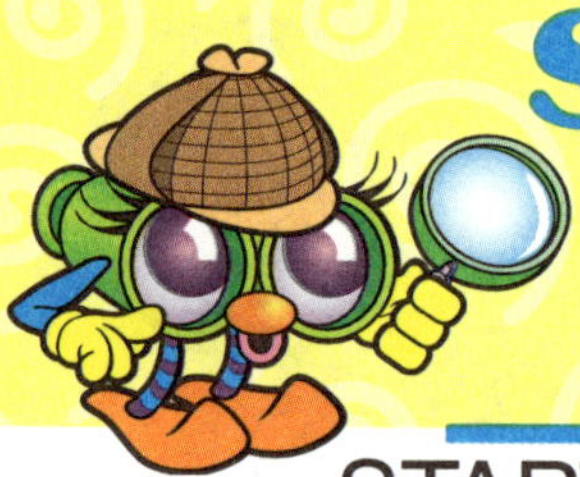

Sight Word Detective

as, at, be, by, but, can

Follow the word *be* from start to finish.

START

be	by	as	can	but
be	by	at	as	can
be	be	but	as	can
at	be	be	be	FINISH

Trace the words. How many times do you see each sight word in the puzzle?

as ☐	by ☐	but ☐
at ☐	be ☐	can ☐

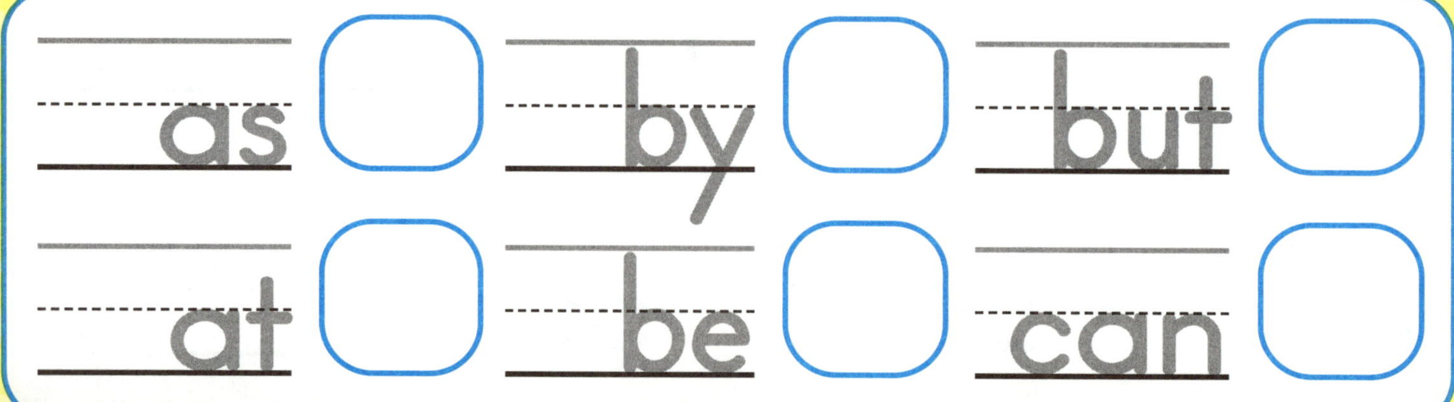

Name:_________________________________

Writing Sight Words

do, each, for, from, go, have

Trace each sight word.
Write the sight word.
Circle the sight word that is different in each row.

do   do   go

for   from   for

each   have   have

Sight Word Search

do, each, for, from, go, have

Find the sight words and circle them in the word search.

d	a	e	a	c	h	i	g
o	f	a	r	e	a	t	o
p	o	m	e	y	v	u	w
w	r	n	p	m	e	m	e
f	r	o	m	c	b	a	z

Write each sight word below as you find it in the puzzle.
Read the words to yourself as you write them.

Find the Odd Word

here, his, if, in, is, my

Circle the sight word that is different from the others in the row.
Write the odd word on the line.
Name the sight word as you write it.

my	if	my	_________
here	here	his	_________
in	if	if	_________
in	in	is	_________
here	my	here	_________
is	is	here	_________

Name: ______________________________

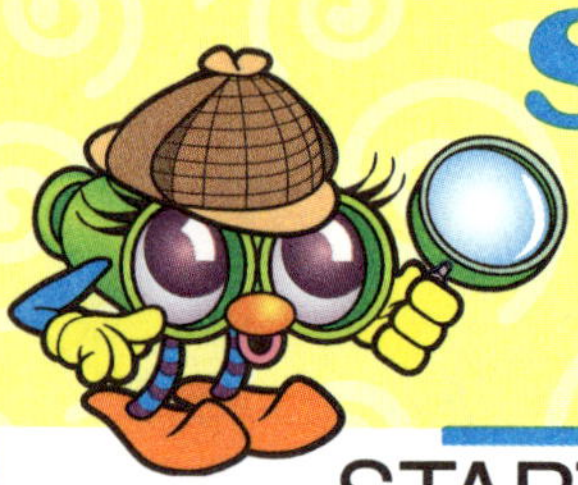

Sight Word Detective

here, his, if, in, is, my

Follow the word *is* from start to finish.

START

is	if	in	my	here
is	if	in	his	in
is	his	here	my	his
is	is	is	is	FINISH

Trace the words. How many times do you see each sight word in the puzzle?

here	☐	if	☐	my	☐
his	☐	in	☐	is	☐

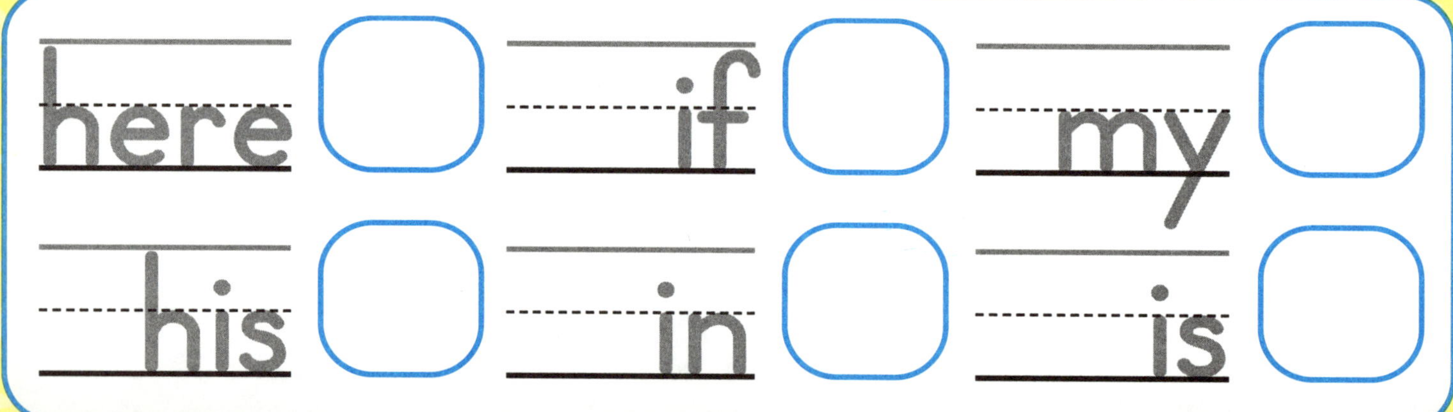

Color the Word

no, not, of, on, play, said

Color the balloons using the code.

Code
no—red
not—blue
of—yellow
on—purple
play—green
said—orange

Center Note: Students can use colored dry erase pens or colored, transparent bingo chips to mark this sheet.

Name: ______________________________

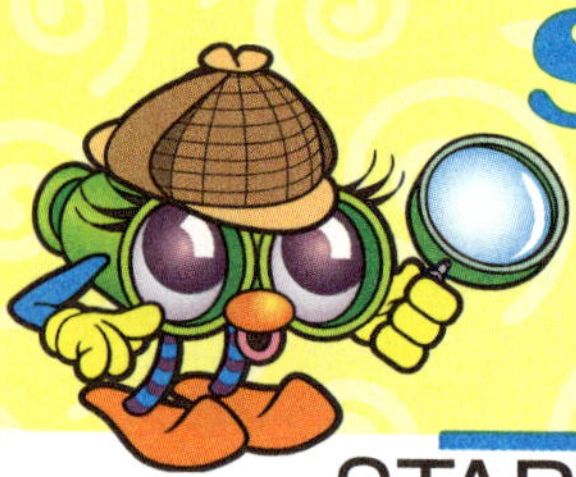

Sight Word Detective

no, not, of, on, play, said

Follow the word *not* from start to finish.

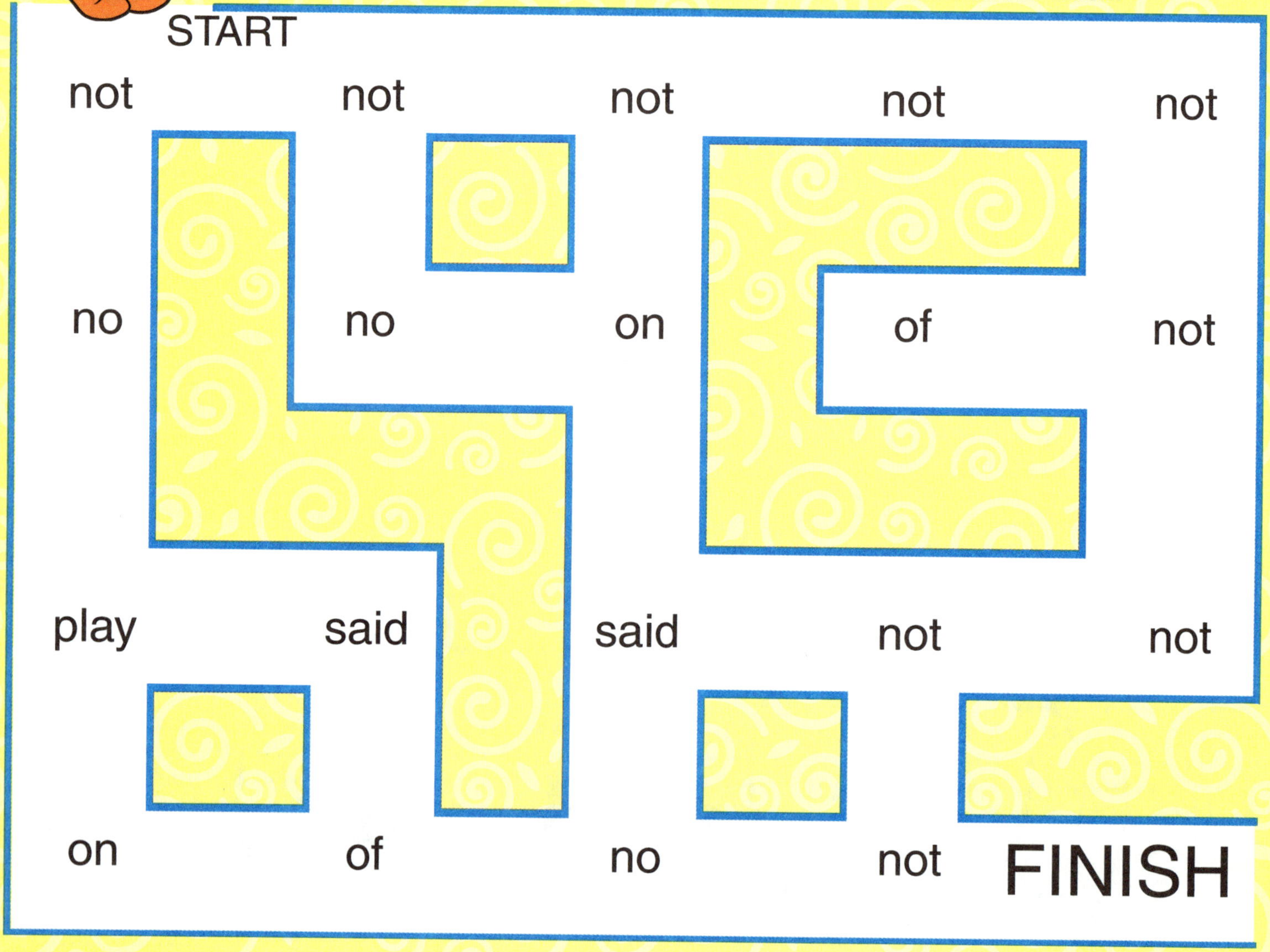

START
not not not not not
no no on of not
play said said not not
on of no not
FINISH

Trace the words. How many times do you see each sight word in the puzzle?

no ☐ of ☐ play ☐

not ☐ on ☐ said ☐

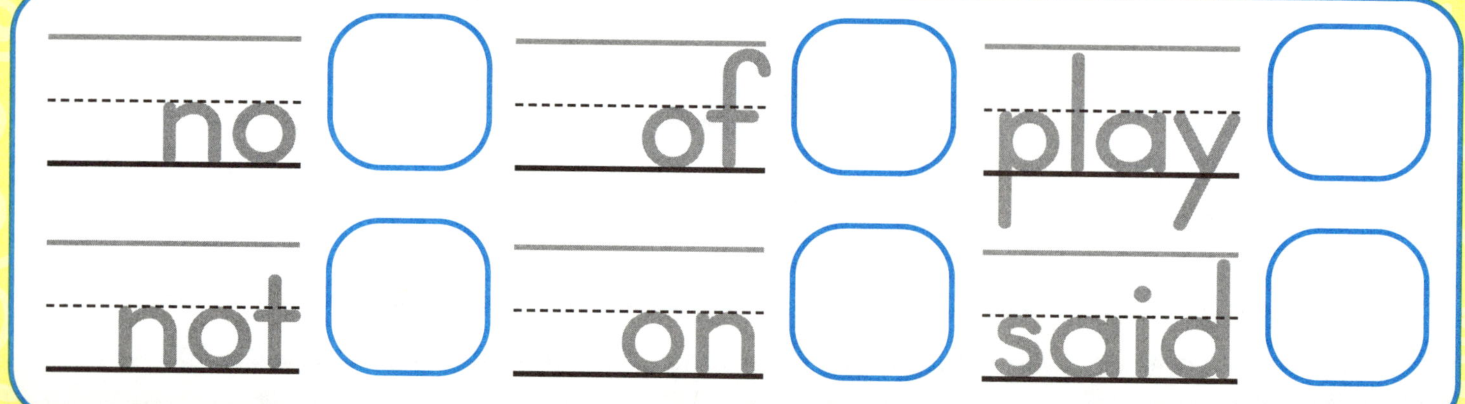

Picture It

see, stop, that, the, there, their

Cross out the picture that does not match the word. Write the word.

see 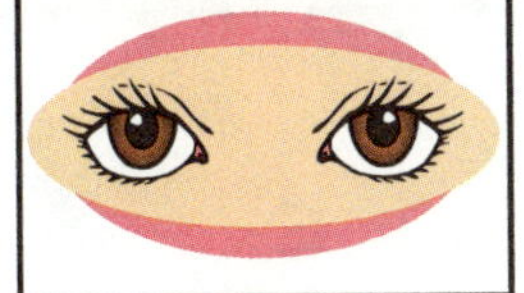  ____________

stop 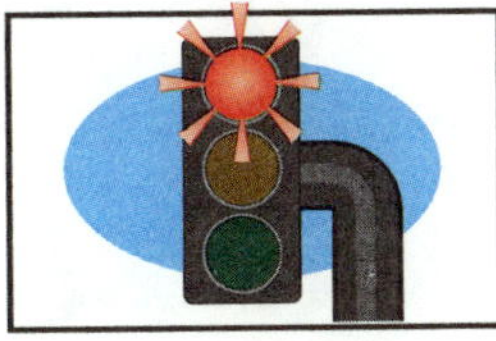  ____________

Trace and write these sight words. Name the sight word as you write it.

that that ____________

the the ____________

there there ____________

their their ____________

Sight Word Search

see, stop, that, the, there, their

Find the sight words and circle them in the word search.

Write each sight word below as you find it in the puzzle.
Read the words to yourself as you write them.

Match Up

this, to, up, was, were, your

Draw a line to match the sight words. Write the sight words in the box at the bottom.

your

were

this

up

was

up

your

to

were

to

this

was

Sight Word Detective

this, to, up, was, were, your

Follow the word *were* from start to finish.

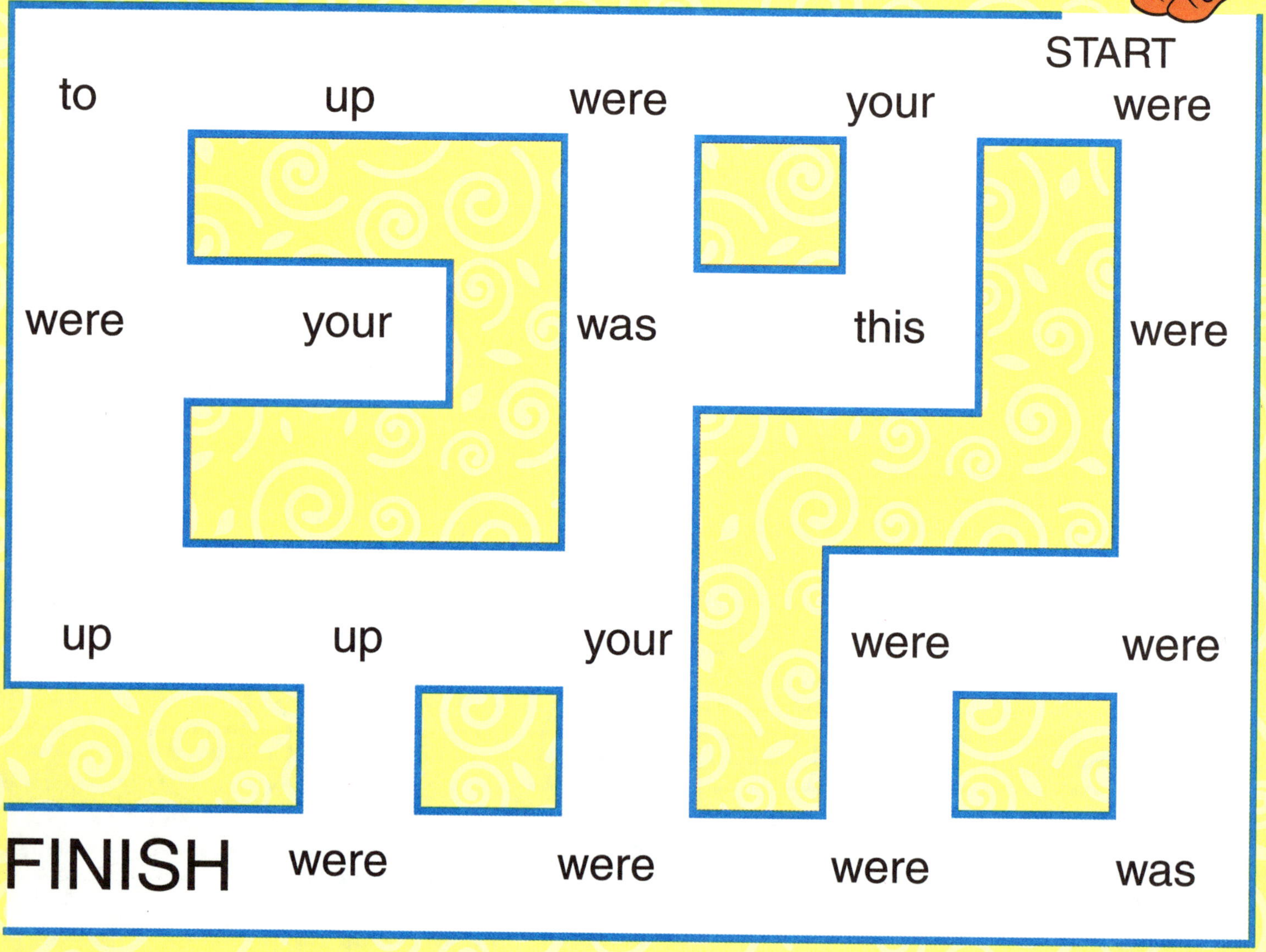

START

to	up	were	your	were
were	your	was	this	were
up	up	your	were	were
FINISH	were	were	were	was

Trace the words. How many times do you see each sight word in the puzzle?

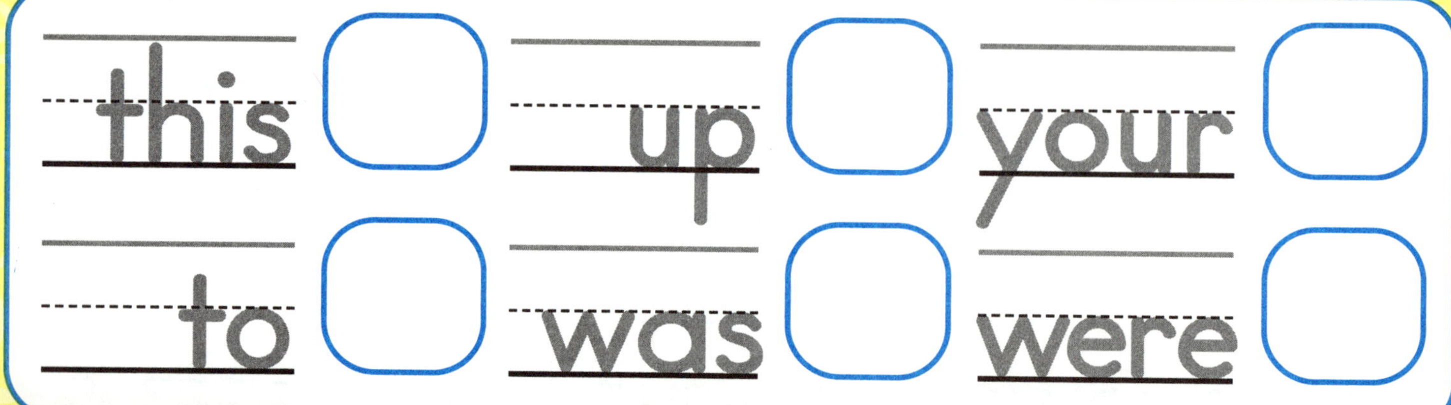

Who Is It?

he, I, it, she, they, we, you

Cut out the pronouns. Glue or place the words in the box next to the correct picture.

he	you	it
she	they	we

Name: ______________________________

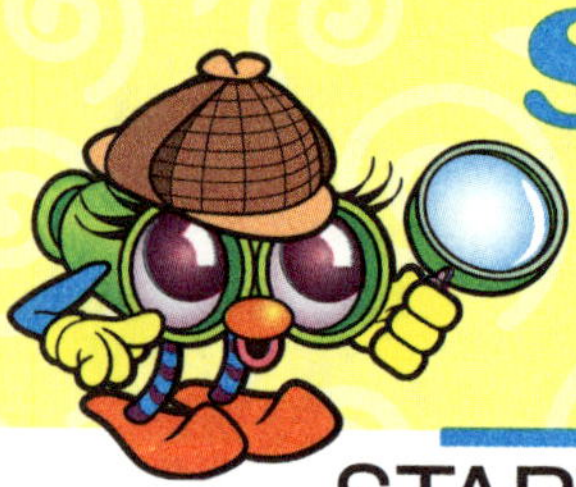

Sight Word Detective

he, it, they, we, you, she

Follow the word *he* from start to finish.

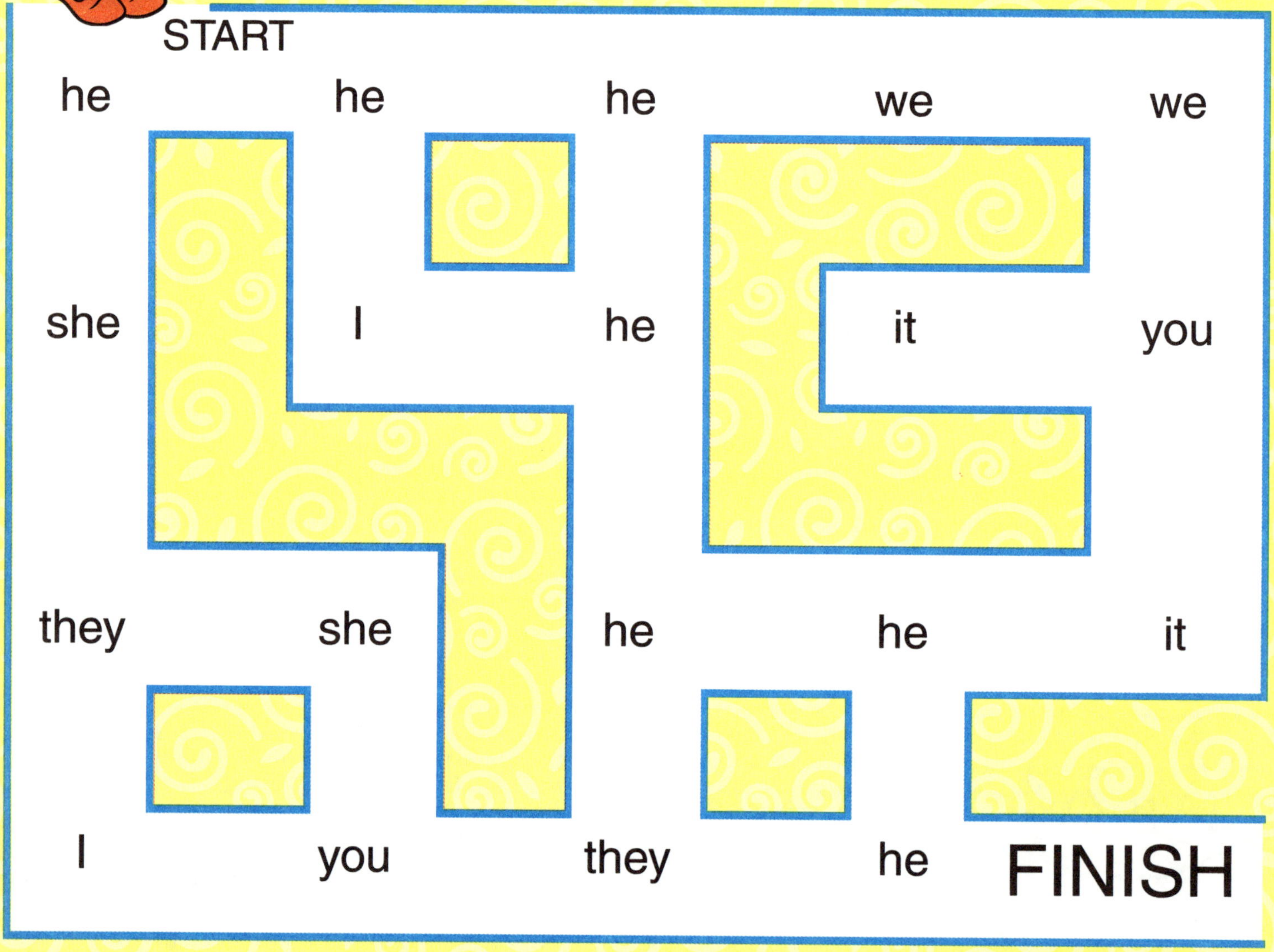

START
he he he we we
she I he it you
they she he he it
I you they he
FINISH

Trace the words. How many times do you see each sight word in the puzzle?

he	☐	they	☐	you	☐
it	☐	we	☐	she	☐

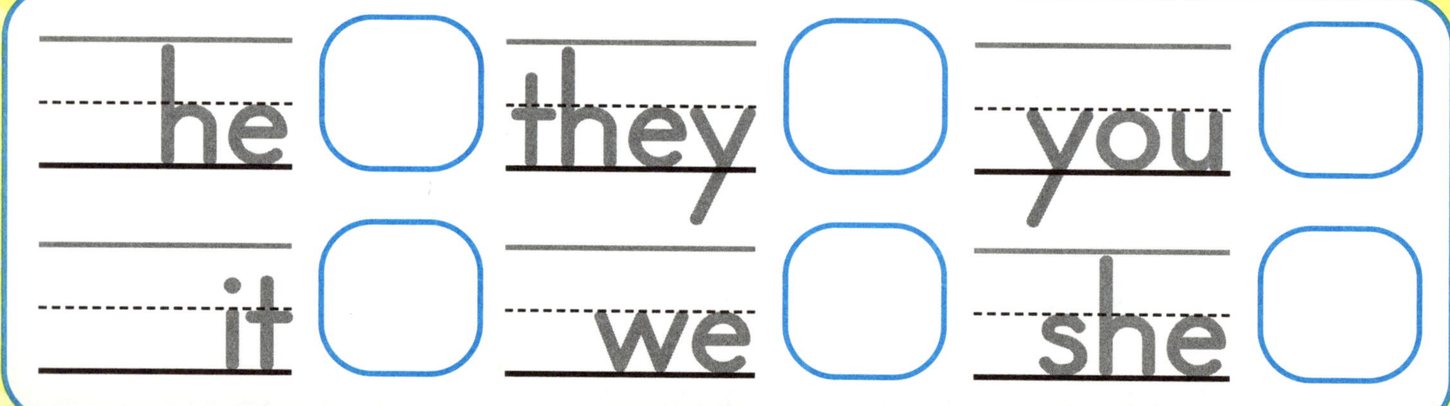

What Color Is It?

black, brown, gray, green

Color the animals using the four colors. Write the color word to complete the sentence.

A skunk can be _______________.

An elephant can be _______________.

A snake can be _______________.

A frog can be _______________.

A bear can be _______________.

A donkey can be _______________.

A horse can be _______________.

A dog can be _______________.

Name: ________________________________

Colorful Flowers

blue, orange, pink, purple, red, yellow, white

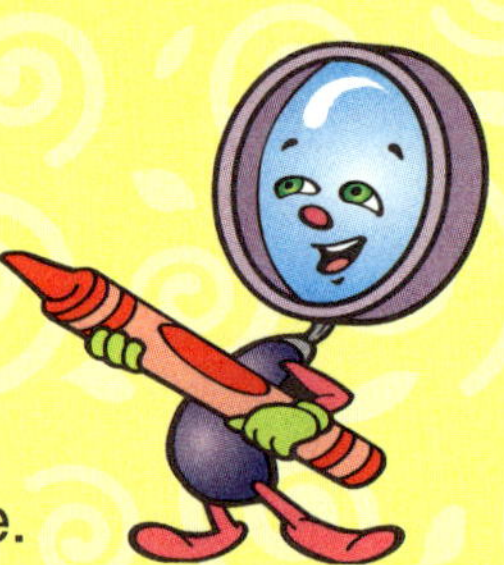

Read the color words in each flower. Color the flowers according to their color name.

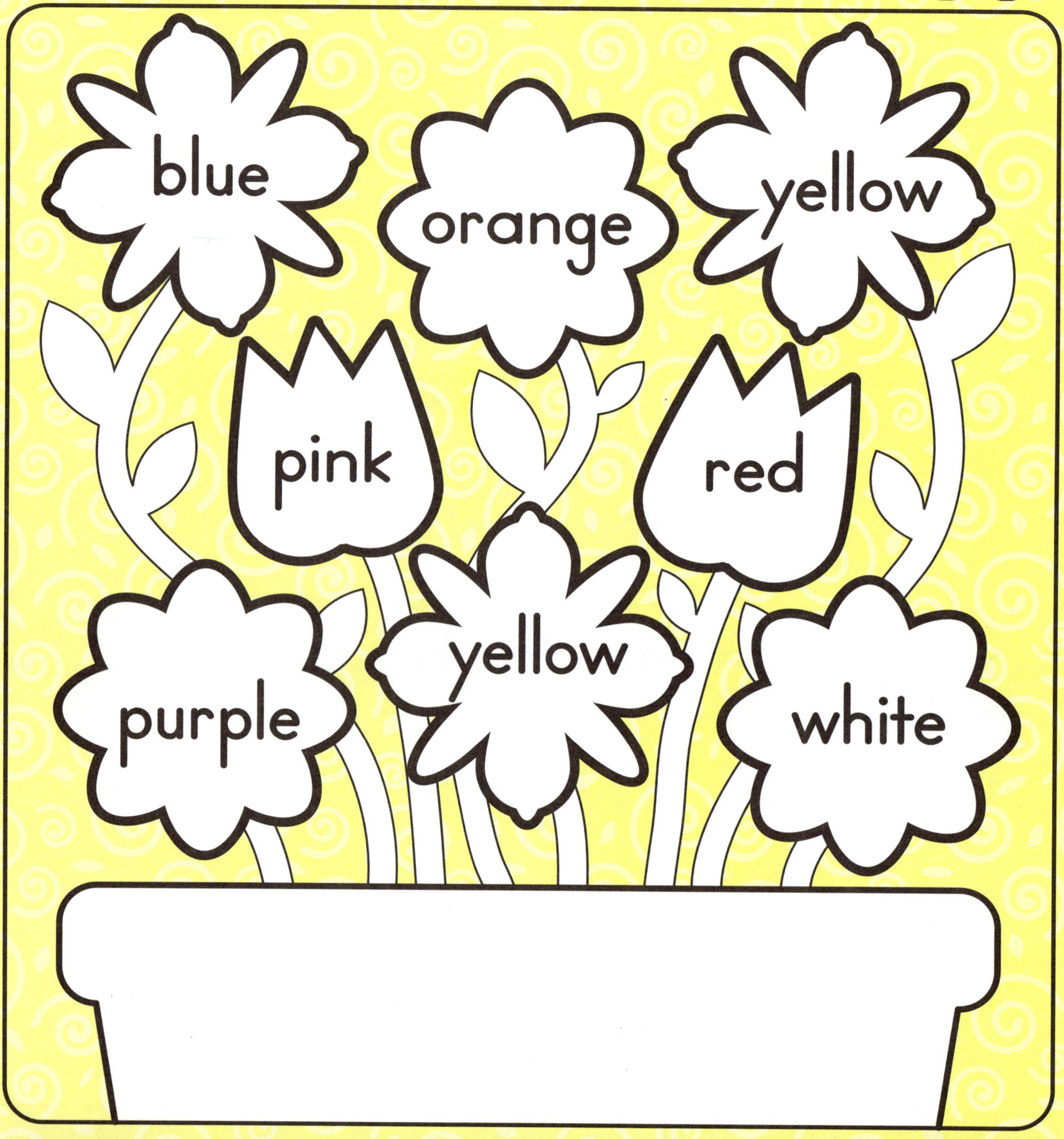

Name: ______________________________

They Look Alike

was, is, saw

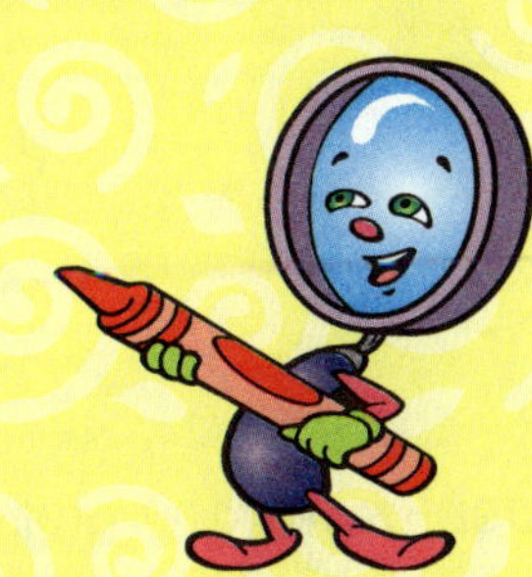

Use *orange* to color all the stars with the word **was** written inside.

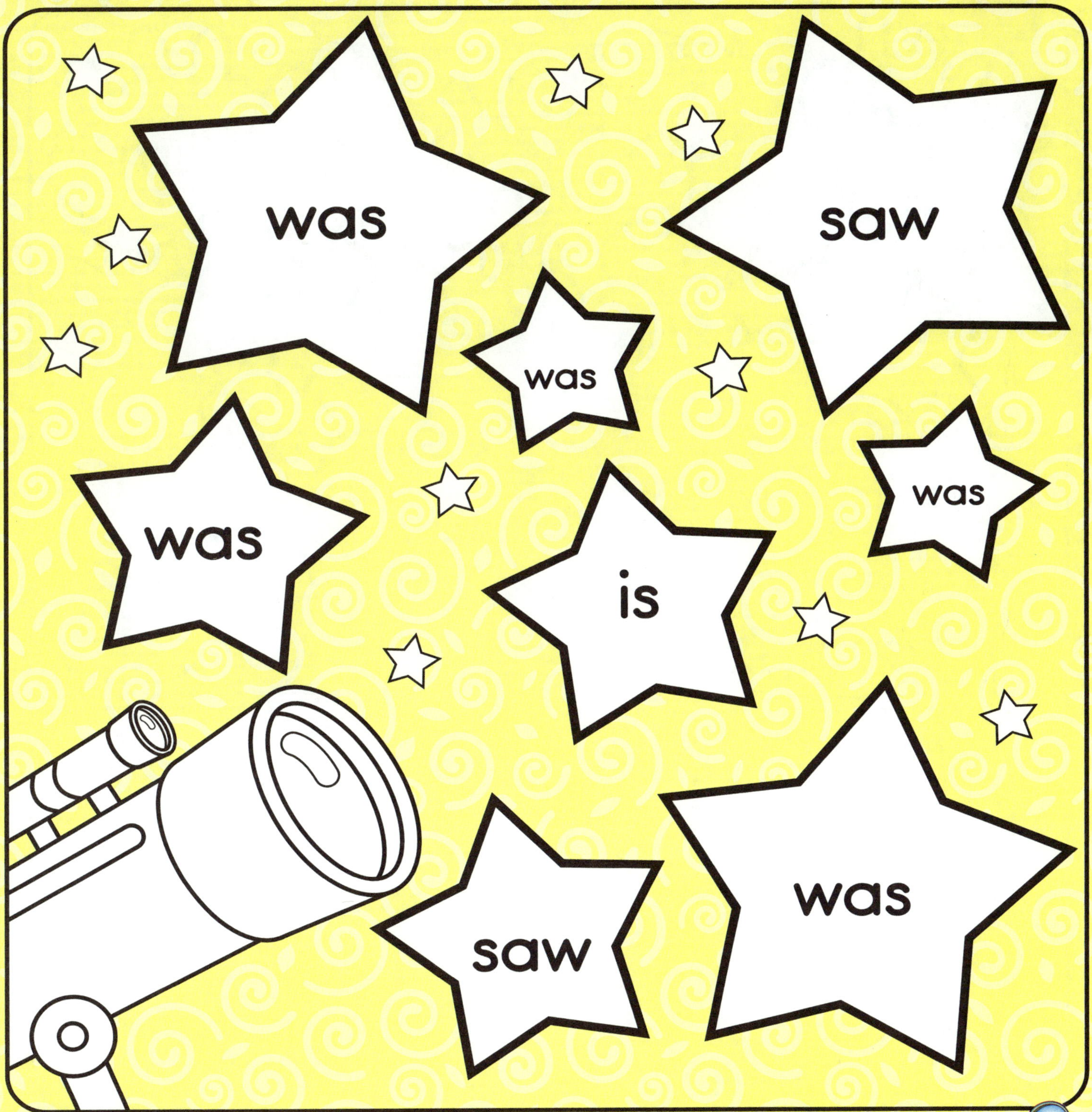

Center Note: Use different colored, transparent bingo chips to mark each word.

Name: ____________________

They Look Alike

an, am, and

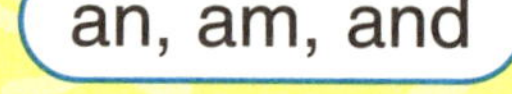

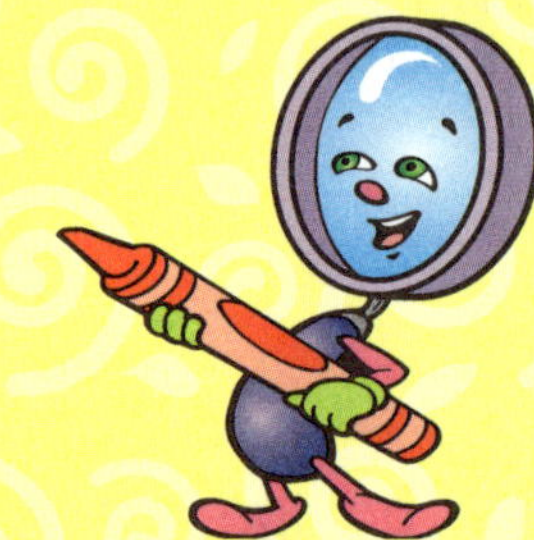

Use *brown* to color all the bugs with the word **am** written inside.

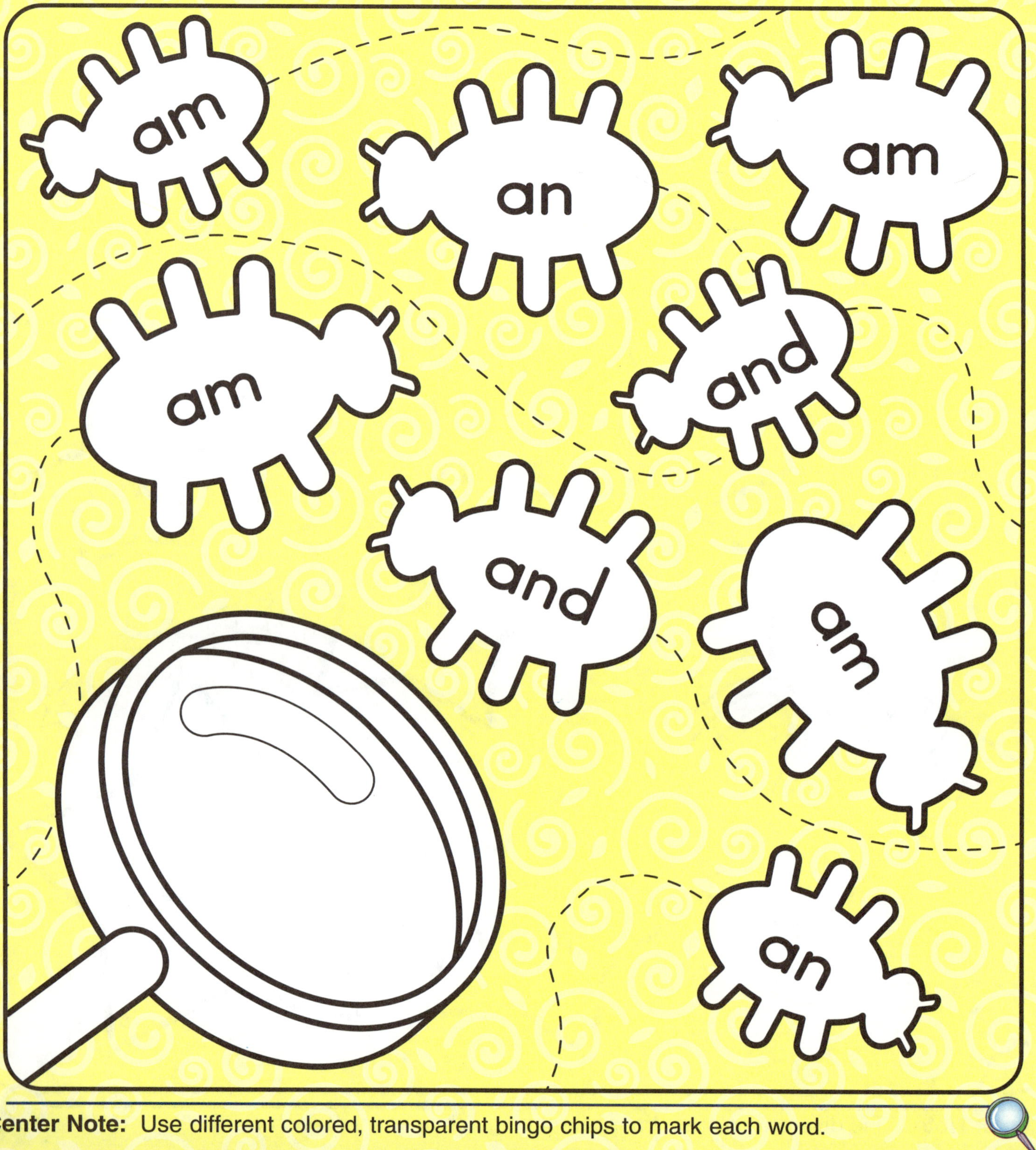

Center Note: Use different colored, transparent bingo chips to mark each word.

Sort them Out

is, his, this

Cut the words apart. Place them in the correct box.

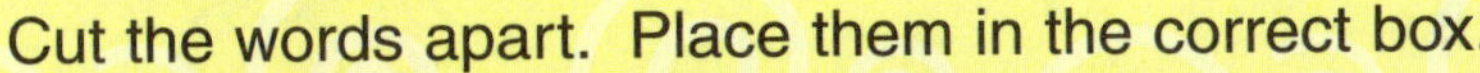

is	this	his	his
this	this	is	his

Center Note: Cut and laminate the small pieces. Store in a resealable bag.

©*Teacher Created Resources, Inc.* 145 *#3174 Literacy Centers for Sight Words*

Sort Them Out

that, the, there

Cut the words apart. Place them in the correct house.

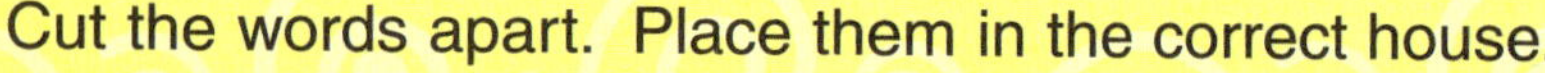

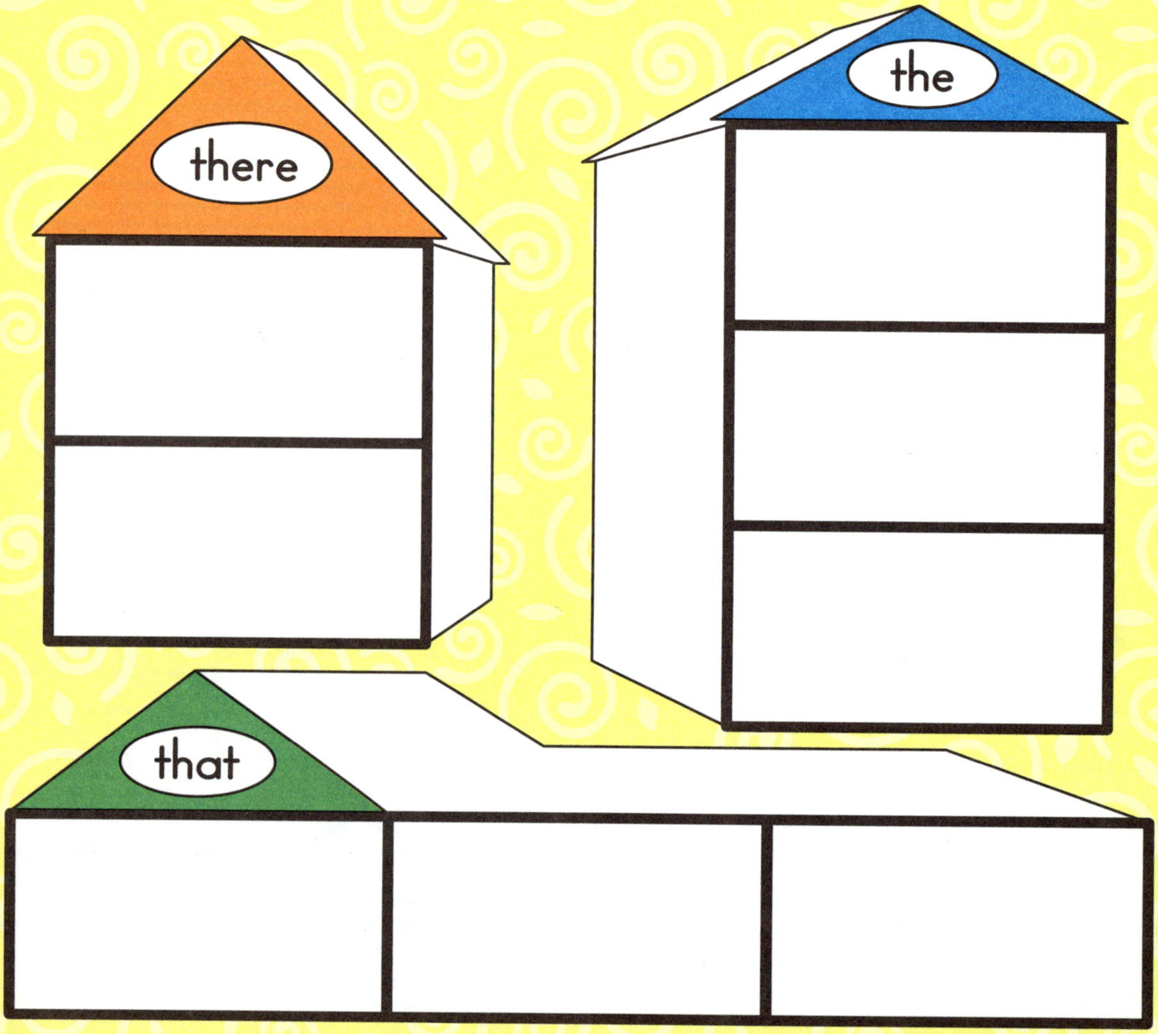

| that | there | the | the |
| that | the | that | there |

Center Note: Cut and laminate the small pieces. Store in a resealable bag.

Word Families

—am

Cut out the letters and glue them in the correct box to make the words match the pictures. Write the new word on the line.

am

am

am

am

h y r j

Center Note: Cut and laminate the small pieces. Store in a resealable bag.

Name: ___________________________

Word Families

—an

Cut out the letters and glue them in the correct box to make the
words match the pictures. Write the new word on the line.

	an

____

	an

____

	an

____

	an

____

f	c	p	m

Center Note: Cut and laminate the small pieces. Store in a resealable bag.

Word Families

—all

Cut out the letters and glue them in the correct box to make the words match the pictures. Write the new word on the line.

all

all

all

all

| c | f | b | w |

Center Note: Cut and laminate the small pieces. Store in a resealable bag.

Word Families

—at

Cut out the letters and glue them in the correct box to make the words match the pictures. Write the new word on the line.

	at
	at
	at
	at

| r | b | c | h |

Center Note: Cut and laminate the small pieces. Store in a resealable bag.

Word Families

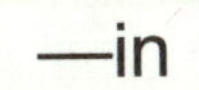

—in

Cut out the letters and glue them in the correct box to make the words match the pictures. Write the word on the line.

	in

____

	in

____

	in

____

	in

____

f	p	t	ch

Center Note: Cut and laminate the small pieces. Store in a resealable bag.

Word Families

Cut out the words and place them in the correct word family frame.

Center Note: Cut and laminate the small pieces. Store in a resealable bag.

Sentence Cards

Teacher Directions: Cut apart the sentence cards (pages 153–155) and laminate them. Use the picture cards (page 157) and the color word cards (page 159) to complete these sentences.

is

is

the

My

See

That

Teacher Created Resources

Sentence Cards

Teacher Directions: Cut apart the sentence cards (pages 153–155) and laminate them. Use the picture cards (page 157) and the color word cards (page 159) to complete these sentences.

is

was

is

A

His

That

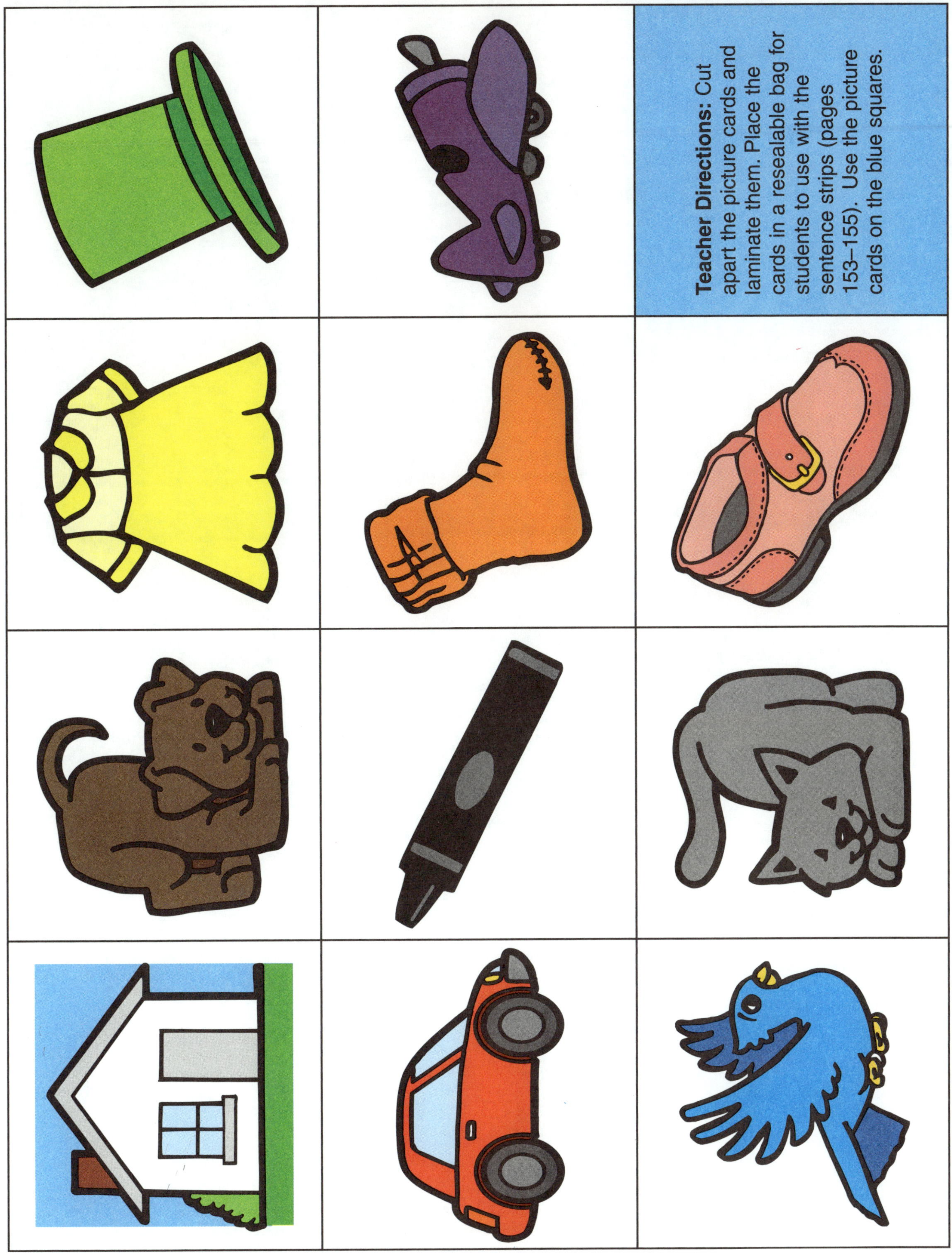
Teacher Directions: Cut apart the picture cards and laminate them. Place the cards in a resealable bag for students to use with the sentence strips (pages 153–155). Use the picture cards on the blue squares.

Gray

Purple

Brown

Pink

Yellow

Blue

Orange

White

Black

Green

Red

Sight Word Master Game

Game Instructions

For 2–4 players

Objective

Make your way along the path reading, spelling, and using sight words in sentences. If you successfully make your way through to the finish, you are on your way to becoming a Sight Word Master!

Equipment

- Game Board (pages 171–173)
- Word Cards (pages 163–167)
- player pieces and spinner (page 169)
- resealable bag or container for storage (not provided)

*For durability, laminate the direction card, game board, spinner, game pieces, and word cards.

Setup

Choose appropriate word cards. Shuffle the word cards to be used and place them in a pile, facedown on one side of the game board. Place the spinner on the other side of the game board. (A paper clip can be used as the "spinner.") Place all player pieces at the start.

How to Play

1. Choose a player to go first. Play will pass to the left.

2. Spin the spinner and move the number of spaces indicated. If you spin to move backward on your first turn, simply spin again.

3. Take a new card each turn. Complete the activities as follows.

   Read: Turn the top card over and read the sight word.

   Spell: Have the person to your left pick up the top card and not show it to you. Have him or her read the sight word, and you say the letters to spell the words. (e.g., "HE, H, E")

   Use It: Turn the top card over and read the word silently to yourself. Think of a sentence in which you can use that word. Say the sentence out loud. (e.g., "HE, He is in my class.")

   Choose: Turn over the top card and choose your favorite activity. If you cannot complete the task, you must return to where you started. You may ask any of the other players to give you the answer, so you will be ready the next time the card comes up. When you run out of word cards, reshuffle them and place them in a pile face down again.

Winning

When a player gets to the Finish square, he or she has won. An exact roll is not needed.

Sight Word Master

Word Cards

a	all	am
an	and	are
as	at	be
by	but	can
do	each	for

Sight Word Master

Sight Word Master

Sight Word Master

Sight Word Master

Sight Word Master

Sight Word Master

Sight Word Master

Sight Word Master

Sight Word Master

Sight Word Master

Sight Word Master

Sight Word Master

Sight Word Master

Sight Word Master

Sight Word Master

©Teacher Created Resources, Inc.

Sight Word Master

Word Cards

from	go	have
here	his	if
in	is	my
no	not	of
on	play	said

Sight
Word
Master

Sight
Word
Master

Sight
Word
Master

Sight
Word
Master

Sight
Word
Master

Sight
Word
Master

Sight
Word
Master

Sight
Word
Master

Sight
Word
Master

Sight
Word
Master

Sight
Word
Master

Sight
Word
Master

Sight
Word
Master

Sight
Word
Master

Sight
Word
Master

Sight Word Master

Word Cards

see	stop	that
the	there	their
this	to	up
was	were	your
he	I	it

Sight Word Master	Sight Word Master	Sight Word Master
Sight Word Master	Sight Word Master	Sight Word Master
Sight Word Master	Sight Word Master	Sight Word Master
Sight Word Master	Sight Word Master	Sight Word Master
Sight Word Master	Sight Word Master	Sight Word Master

Sight Word Master

Word Cards

she	they	we
you	black	blue
brown	gray	green
orange	pink	purple
red	white	yellow

Sight
Word
Master

Sight
Word
Master

Sight
Word
Master

Sight
Word
Master

Sight
Word
Master

Sight
Word
Master

Sight
Word
Master

Sight
Word
Master

Sight
Word
Master

Sight
Word
Master

Sight
Word
Master

Sight
Word
Master

Sight
Word
Master

Sight
Word
Master

Sight
Word
Master

Sight Word Master Game

Teacher
Created
Resources

Teacher
Created
Resources

Teacher
Created
Resources

Teacher
Created
Resources

Teacher
Created
Resources

Teacher
Created
Resources

Teacher
Created
Resources

Teacher
Created
Resources

Teacher
Created
Resources

Teacher
Created
Resources

Teacher
Created
Resources

Teacher
Created
Resources

Teacher
Created
Resources

Teacher
Created
Resources

Teacher
Created
Resources

Teacher
Created
Resources

Teacher
Created
Resources

Teacher
Created
Resources

Teacher
Created
Resources

Teacher
Created
Resources

Teacher
Created
Resources

Teacher
Created
Resources

Teacher
Created
Resources

Teacher
Created
Resources

Teacher
Created
Resources

Teacher
Created
Resources

Teacher
Created
Resources

Teacher
Created
Resources

Teacher
Created
Resources

Teacher
Created
Resources

Teacher
Created
Resources

Teacher
Created
Resources

Sight Word Master

START
Read
Spell
Read
Use It
Choose
Do Two 2
Spell
c-a-t
Read
Choose
Read
Spell
c-a-t
FINISH